Journey
to the
Heart

Journey to the Heart

A Guide to Prayer, Resilience, and Spiritual Growth

Roxie Dantzler

Library of Congress Control Number:		2024916694
ISBN:	Hardcover	979-8-3694-2755-2
	Softcover	979-8-3694-2753-8
	eBook	979-8-3694-2754-5

Print information available on the last page.

Rev. date: 08/15/2024

To order additional copies of this book, contact:
Xlibris
844-714-8691
www.Xlibris.com
Orders@Xlibris.com
861481

Dedication

To all those who are seeking a deeper connection, peace, and understanding through the transformative power of prayer, may this book serve as a guiding light on your spiritual journey, illuminating the path to a deeper relationship with the divine and a more profound sense of inner peace.

To my father, whom I lost in 2016, your unwavering support and love have been a constant source of strength and inspiration throughout my life. Your belief in me has been my bedrock, and your encouragement has fueled my passion for exploring and sharing the depths of spiritual practice. Without your love and support, this book would not have been possible.

To my family and the mentors I have had along the way, who have illuminated my path and nurtured my soul with their wisdom, guidance, and compassion, your teachings have shaped my understanding of prayer and spirituality, and your example has inspired me to delve deeper into my faith. I am eternally grateful for your influence and the profound impact you have had on my life.

And to the readers of this book—may your journey of prayer bring you closer to the divine and to your true self. I hope that the practices, reflections, and insights shared within these pages enrich your spiritual life and provide you with the tools to navigate life's challenges with grace and resilience. May you find comfort, strength, and joy in your connection with the divine.

With heartfelt gratitude and blessings,

Roxie Dantzler

Contents

Foreword

When I first met Ms. Roxie Dantzler, I was immediately struck by her passion for spiritual growth and her dedication to finding healing and enlightenment. Her unique background and experiences have given her an exceptional understanding of the human spirit and its capacity for resilience. As we discussed various spiritual topics, her awareness and enthusiasm to learn more became very evident.

In this book, Roxie presents a practical and inspiring guide for anyone seeking a deeper spiritual connection. Her approach to prayer and spiritual practice is both accessible and insightful, providing readers with the tools they need to navigate life's challenges with grace and strength.

Having been raised in a spiritual family, I feel deeply honored to write the foreword for this remarkable book. This book will undoubtedly resonate with readers from all backgrounds and walks of life, offering a significant source of comfort, guidance, and inspiration. Through Roxie's willingness to learn, she has created a sense of connection and support, making this book a valuable resource on anyone's spiritual journey.

I wholeheartedly recommend this book to anyone seeking to enhance their spiritual journey. It is a testament to Roxie's dedication, compassion, and understanding of how powerful prayer can be. This book will surely guide and assist you on your own spiritual path.

Alex Pinckney

Preface

Writing this book has been an extraordinary journey of discovery and growth. It all began during a personal healing journey that profoundly transformed my life. Through this process, I encountered moments of deep reflection, resilience, and spiritual awakening. These experiences inspired me to share the insights and wisdom I gained with others who may be on similar paths.

The purpose of this book is to offer guidance and support to those seeking a deeper connection with the divine, inner peace, and personal growth. Throughout these pages, you will find a blend of prayer practices, reflections, and practical exercises designed to help you navigate your spiritual journey with grace and resilience.

As you read, I invite you to explore the various themes and practices presented and to integrate them into your own life in a way that feels meaningful and authentic. My hope is that this book serves as a companion and source of inspiration, providing you with the tools and encouragement needed to deepen your spiritual practice and connect more profoundly with the divine.

Thank you for joining me on this journey. May this book illuminate your path and bring you closer to the peace, joy, and understanding that comes from a deep and abiding connection with the divine.

With heartfelt gratitude,

Roxie Dantzler

Acknowledgments

Writing this book has been a journey of discovery and growth, and it would not have been possible without the support and encouragement of many wonderful individuals.

First and foremost, I would like to extend my deepest gratitude to my family for their unwavering support and love throughout this entire journey. Though I may not have mentioned in detail that I was writing this book, you often heard the constant typing away in the late-night hours. I wanted the finished product to be a surprise to you and a birthday gift to myself. Completing this book is a testament to my personal growth, perseverance, and dedication to exploring and sharing the depths of spiritual practice.

A special acknowledgment goes to my father, whom I lost in 2016. Your unwavering support and love have been the bedrock of my life. Your belief in me and your encouragement fueled my passion for exploring and sharing the depths of spiritual practice. Though you are no longer with us, your spirit and legacy continue to inspire and guide me every day. Your belief in me has been my greatest source of strength and inspiration, providing the foundation upon which this book was built. In my life, every step of the way, you have stood by me, offering words of wisdom, moments of comfort, and endless motivation. Without your unwavering support, this book would not have been possible. Thank you for being my constant source of encouragement and for believing in my dreams, even when they seemed distant.

I am deeply grateful to my mentors, whose wisdom and guidance have illuminated my path. Your teachings have profoundly shaped my understanding of prayer and spirituality, and I am honored to have learned from you. My mentors' invaluable assistance and guidance have been instrumental in the creation of this book. Your support has helped shape and refine my ideas, and for that, I am profoundly grateful.

I would also like to extend my gratitude to my editor, whose keen eye and thoughtful suggestions have greatly improved this book. Your dedication and expertise have been essential in bringing this project to life.

Finally, to my readers, thank you for taking on this journey with me. I hope this book brings you as much joy and enlightenment as it has brought me in writing it.

With heartfelt gratitude,

Roxie Dantzler

Introduction

Welcome to a Journey of the Heart

In the hustle and bustle of our daily lives, we often find ourselves yearning for moments of peace, clarity, and connection. It is in these moments that we turn inward, seeking a source of strength and solace that transcends the mundane. This book is a guide to that sacred practice: prayer.

The Purpose of This Book

Prayer has been a cornerstone of human existence for millennia, a bridge between the earthly and the divine, a conversation that brings us closer to the essence of our being and to the greater universe. The purpose of this book is to explore the multifaceted dimensions of prayer, to understand its profound impact on our lives, and to offer practical guidance for those who wish to deepen their spiritual practice.

Prayer is more than just a set of words or rituals; it is a heartfelt communication that allows us to express our deepest longings, gratitude, and concerns. Through prayer, we connect with something greater than ourselves, finding comfort, guidance, and strength. This book seeks to demystify prayer, making it accessible and meaningful for everyone, regardless of their religious or spiritual background.

A Personal Journey

For many, prayer is a deeply personal journey, as it has been for me. My own experiences with prayer have shaped my understanding of its power and its ability to transform lives. Whether in moments of joy or sorrow, triumph or trial, prayer has been a constant companion, a beacon of hope, and a source of unwavering strength. Through this book, I wish to share the insights and lessons I have gathered along the way, hoping to inspire and support others on their own spiritual journeys.

I remember a time when I felt lost and overwhelmed, unsure of the path ahead. It was during these moments of uncertainty that I turned to prayer, seeking solace and guidance. As I poured out my heart, I felt a profound sense of peace wash over me, reassuring me that I was not alone. This experience, and many others like it, has taught me the invaluable role that prayer can play in our lives.

Scope and Structure

This book is designed to be a comprehensive guide, covering various aspects of prayer and its practice. I will begin with an exploration of what prayer is, delving into its definitions, historical context, and different forms. I will then examine the importance of prayer, highlighting its spiritual, emotional, and communal benefits.

In my journey through the chapters, I will explore the rich tapestry of prayer traditions across different cultures and religions. By understanding the diverse ways in which people pray, I can appreciate the universality of this practice and its ability to transcend boundaries. From the ancient chants of indigenous tribes to the solemn prayers of monastic communities, each form of prayer carries its unique beauty and significance.

For those looking to establish or enhance their prayer practice, I will provide practical tips on creating a sacred space, developing a routine, and overcoming common challenges. I will also offer a collection of prayers for different occasions, personal stories of how prayer has impacted lives, and insights from various religious and cultural traditions.

Creating a sacred space for prayer is essential in fostering a deep and meaningful connection. Whether it's a quiet corner in your home, a garden, or a special room, having a dedicated space can enhance your prayer experience. I will discuss ways to personalize your space, incorporating elements that inspire and uplift you.

Developing a routine is another crucial aspect of maintaining a consistent prayer practice. I will explore different approaches to integrating prayer into your daily life, making it a natural and enriching part of your routine. From morning prayers to evening reflections, I will provide guidance on finding a rhythm that works for you.

Finally, I will encourage readers to create their own prayers, incorporating personal reflections, scriptures, and poetry. The book will also include sections on keeping a prayer journal and engaging in reflective practices to deepen the prayer experience. A prayer journal can serve as a powerful tool for documenting your spiritual journey, allowing you to reflect on your prayers, insights, and experiences over time.

An Invitation

As you begin this journey through the pages of this book, I invite you to open your heart and mind to the transformative power of prayer. Whether you are new to prayer or seeking to deepen your existing practice, may this book serve as a source of inspiration, guidance, and support. Together, let us explore the sacred art of prayer and discover the profound peace, strength, and connection it can bring into our lives.

In the coming chapters, I will explore the rich history of prayer, uncovering its timeless significance and relevance in our modern world. I will share stories from individuals whose lives have been touched by prayer, recounting their tales of hope, healing, and transformation. Through these narratives, I will illustrate the miraculous ways in which prayer can shape our lives and the lives of those around us.

This book is not just a manual; it is an invitation to begin a sacred journey. As you read, I encourage you to reflect on your own experiences with prayer and to experiment with different forms and practices. Allow yourself the freedom to explore and to discover what resonates with you."

May this book be a companion on your spiritual path, offering wisdom, encouragement, and inspiration. May it help you cultivate a deeper connection with the divine and with your own inner self. And may it remind you that, no matter where you are on your journey, you are never alone.

Blessings to you on this sacred journey.

Chapter 1

Understanding Prayer

Definition of Prayer

Prayer is a universal act of communication with the divine, the sacred, or a higher power. It transcends cultures, religions, and epochs, embodying a deep human need to connect, seek guidance, express gratitude, and find solace. At its core, prayer is a conversation—a dialogue that bridges the gap between the human and the divine.

Prayer can be understood in various ways depending on individual beliefs and traditions. For some, it is a formal ritual recited at specific times, while for others, it is a spontaneous expression of thoughts and emotions. Despite these differences, the essence of prayer remains the same: it is an intentional act of reaching out beyond oneself, seeking a connection with something greater.

This connection can be deeply personal, tailored to the unique experiences and spiritual inclinations of the individual. For instance, someone may find solace in the structured prayers of their religious tradition, reciting words that have been passed down through generations. Others may prefer the freedom of speaking from the heart, expressing their thoughts and feelings in a more fluid and spontaneous manner.

Moreover, prayer is not confined to words alone. It can be expressed through silence, song, movement, or art. The act of creating a piece of music, painting a picture, or simply sitting in quiet reflection can all be forms of prayer. These diverse expressions highlight the flexibility and inclusivity of prayer as a spiritual practice, making it accessible to everyone, regardless of their background or beliefs.

Historical Context

The practice of prayer is as old as humanity itself. Archaeological evidence suggests that ancient civilizations engaged in prayer and ritualistic worship to honor their gods and seek their favor. From the sacred chants of the ancient Egyptians to the Vedic hymns of early Indian civilization, prayer has been a fundamental aspect of religious life across the globe.

In ancient Mesopotamia, people prayed to a pantheon of gods, each overseeing different aspects of life. The Greeks and Romans also had elaborate systems of prayer and offerings to their deities, reflecting their desire to influence the gods' favor in their daily lives. Meanwhile, in the east, prayer practices in Hinduism, Buddhism, and other traditions evolved, emphasizing meditation, chanting, and personal devotion.

Throughout history, prayer has played a pivotal role in major world religions. In Christianity, the Lord's Prayer, taught by Jesus to his disciples, remains a central tenet of Christian worship. This prayer, with its simple yet profound words, encapsulates the essence of Christian spirituality, emphasizing themes of forgiveness, provision, and divine guidance. Within Christianity, there are diverse traditions and practices of prayer.

In Catholicism, prayer is deeply intertwined with the sacraments and liturgical life of the Church. The Rosary, a form of prayer using beads, involves meditating on significant events in the life of Jesus and Mary. The Mass, central to Catholic worship, is itself a profound act of communal prayer, where the faithful participate in the Eucharist, offering prayers of adoration, thanksgiving, and supplication.

Famous Quote: "Prayer is the oxygen of the soul" (St. Padre Pio).

Example of a Catholic Prayer (The Hail Mary)

"Hail Mary, full of grace, the Lord is with thee. Blessed art thou among women, and blessed is the fruit of thy womb, Jesus. Holy Mary, Mother of God, pray for us sinners, now and at the hour of our death. Amen."

Protestantism, with its various denominations, also embraces prayer as a vital component of faith. While there is no single structure, Protestant prayers often emphasize personal relationship with God, scriptural reflection, and communal worship. The Book of Common Prayer, used by Anglicans, provides a rich resource of prayers for various occasions, embodying both the communal and personal aspects of prayer.

Famous Quote: "God does nothing but in answer to prayer" (John Wesley).

Example of a Protestant Prayer (from the Book of Common Prayer)

"Almighty and most merciful Father, we have erred and strayed from thy ways like lost sheep. We have followed too much the devices and desires of our own hearts. We have offended against thy holy laws. We have left undone those things which we ought to have done; and we have done those things which we ought not to have done; and there is no health in us. But thou, O Lord, have mercy upon us, miserable offenders. Spare thou those, O God, who confess their faults. Restore thou those who are penitent, according to thy promises declared unto mankind in Christ Jesus our Lord. And grant, O most merciful Father, for his sake, that we may hereafter live a godly, righteous, and sober life, to the glory of thy holy Name. Amen."

In Islam, the five daily prayers (Salah) are a fundamental practice, reinforcing discipline and devotion. These prayers, performed at specific times throughout the day, serve as a constant reminder of the believer's connection to Allah. Judaism, with its rich liturgical traditions, places a significant emphasis on prayer in both communal and personal settings. The prayers in Judaism, often recited in Hebrew, carry deep historical and spiritual significance, connecting the present with the past and the individual with the community.

Historical Event: In 1571, Pope Pius V called for all of Europe to pray the Rosary for victory in the Battle of Lepanto, which ultimately led to a decisive victory for the Holy League against the Ottoman Empire, demonstrating the unifying power of communal prayer.

In indigenous cultures around the world, prayer often takes the form of rituals and ceremonies that honor the natural world and ancestral spirits. For example, Native American traditions include prayers and songs that are integral to ceremonies like the Sun Dance and the Ghost Dance, expressing a deep reverence for the earth and all its inhabitants. These practices underscore the universal nature of prayer as a means of seeking harmony and balance in life.

Buddhism presents a unique perspective on prayer, where the focus is often on meditation and mindfulness rather than direct supplication to a deity. In Buddhism, prayer can take the form of chants and mantras, such as the chanting of "Namo Amituofo" in Pure Land Buddhism or the recitation of the Heart Sutra in Mahayana traditions. These practices are meant to cultivate inner peace, compassion, and wisdom. The act of chanting or reciting mantras serves as a form of meditation, helping practitioners focus their minds and develop spiritual insight.

Famous Quote: "To understand everything is to forgive everything" (Buddha).

Example of a Buddhist Prayer (The Metta Sutta)

"May all beings be happy; may all beings be without disease. May all beings experience the sensation of auspiciousness. May nobody suffer in any way."

Historical Event: In 1959, during the Tibetan uprising, the Dalai Lama and many Tibetans sought refuge in India. Despite the hardship, Tibetan Buddhists continued their practice of prayer and meditation, demonstrating the resilience of their spiritual traditions in the face of adversity.

Types of Prayer

Prayer can take many forms, each serving a unique purpose and reflecting the diverse ways humans seek to connect with the divine. Here are some of the most common types of prayer:

1. Supplication: This is a prayer of request, where individuals ask for help, guidance, or specific needs to be met. It reflects a humble acknowledgment of one's dependence on a higher power. Supplication can be personal, focusing on individual needs, or intercessory, where one prays on behalf of others. In moments of desperation or need, supplication can be a lifeline, providing comfort and hope. It can range from a silent plea in the heart to a collective outpouring of requests in a community setting.

   Example of a Prayer of Supplication
   "Dear God, please give me the strength to face the challenges ahead and the wisdom to make the right decisions. Guide me and protect me in all that I do. Amen."

2. Thanksgiving: Prayers of thanksgiving express gratitude for blessings received. This form of prayer helps cultivate an attitude of thankfulness, recognizing the goodness and generosity of the divine. By regularly engaging in thanksgiving prayers,

individuals can develop a more positive outlook on life, focusing on what they have rather than what they lack. Thanksgiving prayers can be specific, thanking the divine for particular gifts or experiences, or general, expressing overall gratitude for the gift of life itself.

Example of a Prayer of Thanksgiving
"Thank you, Lord, for the many blessings you have given me. Thank you for my family, my health, and the opportunities you provide. Help me to always remember your goodness and to live with a grateful heart. Amen."

3. Intercession: Intercessory prayer involves praying for others, seeking blessings, healing, or intervention on their behalf. It is an act of compassion and solidarity, reflecting a deep concern for the well-being of others. Intercessory prayers can be powerful expressions of love and empathy, uniting people in a shared sense of purpose and care. This type of prayer is often practiced in religious services, prayer groups, or individually, as a way of lifting up the needs of family, friends, and even strangers.

   Example of a Prayer of Intercession
   "Heavenly Father, I lift up my friend who is going through a difficult time. Please comfort and heal them, and give them the strength to overcome their challenges. Surround them with your love and peace. Amen."

4. Adoration: Prayers of adoration are expressions of love and reverence toward the divine. They focus on the greatness, holiness, and majesty of the higher power, fostering a sense of awe and worship. Adoration prayers can be deeply uplifting, helping individuals to transcend their everyday concerns and connect with the sacred. These prayers often involve praising the divine for its attributes, such as omnipotence, wisdom, and benevolence.

Example of a Prayer of Adoration
"O Lord, you are holy and worthy of all praise. Your greatness is beyond measure, and your love is unfailing. I worship you and give you all the glory. Amen."

5. Confession: Confessional prayers involve acknowledging one's faults, sins, and shortcomings before the divine. This type of prayer seeks forgiveness and cleansing, promoting spiritual growth and reconciliation. Through confession, individuals can experience a sense of release and renewal, letting go of guilt and embracing the possibility of transformation. Confessional prayers can be part of regular spiritual practice or special moments of reflection, allowing for honest self-assessment and repentance.

Example of a Prayer of Confession
"Merciful God, I confess that I have sinned against you in thought, word, and deed. I have not loved you with my whole heart, and I have not loved my neighbor as myself. Forgive me, and cleanse me from all unrighteousness. Amen."

6. Meditation: Meditative prayer is a form of silent contemplation, focusing on the presence of the divine. It often involves practices such as breathing exercises, visualization, and the repetition of sacred words or phrases (mantras). Meditation can help individuals achieve a state of inner calm and clarity, fostering a deeper awareness of the divine presence in their lives. This type of prayer is often used in Eastern spiritual traditions and has been adopted in various forms by people seeking a deeper, more introspective prayer experience.

Example of a Meditative Prayer
"As I breathe in, I breathe in peace. As I breathe out, I release tension. I focus on the light within me, and I feel the presence of the divine surrounding me. Om."

7. Contemplation: Contemplative prayer goes beyond words, seeking to experience the divine presence in a deep, intimate way. It is characterized by silent awareness and a profound sense of being in the presence of the sacred. Contemplation can lead to moments of profound insight and connection, offering glimpses of the divine that transcend ordinary experience. This type of prayer is often practiced by mystics and those seeking a deeper union with the divine, emphasizing stillness and inner listening.

Example of a Contemplative Prayer
"I sit in stillness, open and receptive to your presence, O God. In the silence, I feel your love and peace. I rest in your embrace, knowing that you are with me always."

Each type of prayer serves a different purpose and meets different needs, allowing individuals to express their spirituality in various ways. Understanding these forms of prayer can enrich one's spiritual practice, providing a framework for communicating with the divine in meaningful and personal ways.

By exploring the definition, historical context, and various types of prayer, this chapter lays the foundation for a deeper understanding of what prayer is and how it functions in our lives. As you continue reading, you will discover practical ways to incorporate these insights into your own prayer practice, enhancing your spiritual journey.

Prayer is not just a ritual or a tradition; it is a living, dynamic practice that can evolve and grow with you. Whether you are new to prayer or have been praying for years, there is always something new to learn and experience. By approaching prayer with an open heart and mind, you can deepen your connection with the divine and discover new dimensions of your spiritual life.

As you explore the various forms of prayer, you may find that certain types resonate more with you at different times in your life. The flexibility of prayer allows it to adapt to your changing needs and circumstances, offering a source of comfort, guidance, and inspiration whenever you need it.

Chapter 2

The Importance of Prayer

Spiritual Benefits

Prayer is often regarded as the lifeblood of spiritual life, a conduit through which individuals connect with the divine. Its significance extends beyond mere ritual; prayer cultivates a profound sense of spirituality and deepens one's relationship with the sacred. The spiritual benefits of prayer are manifold:

1. Connection with the Divine: Prayer allows individuals to feel connected to a higher power, fostering a sense of companionship and understanding. This connection can provide comfort and reassurance, especially during challenging times.

   Famous Quote: "Prayer is not asking. It is a longing of the soul. It is daily admission of one's weakness. It is better in prayer to have a heart without words than words without a heart" (Mahatma Gandhi).

2. Inner Peace: Engaging in prayer can lead to a state of inner peace and tranquility. It helps calm the mind, reduce stress, and cultivate a sense of serenity. This inner peace is often accompanied by a feeling of being grounded and centered.

Example Prayer for Peace
"Dear God, grant me the serenity to accept the things I cannot change, the courage to change the things I can, and the wisdom to know the difference. Amen."

Personal Anecdote: Finding Inner Peace Through Prayer

A few years ago, I found myself in the midst of a particularly stressful period at work. Every day felt like a race against time, and the pressure was mounting. I would wake up with a sense of dread, my mind already racing with the tasks ahead, and go to bed with a knot of anxiety in my stomach.

The job was especially challenging due to the high turnover rate in my section, which significantly increased my workload. I witnessed the morale of my colleagues plummet as we struggled to keep up with the demands. Management seemed indifferent to our plight, showing little concern for the well-being of some employees. This lack of support made the environment even more taxing.

One evening, after a particularly grueling day, I decided to take a break and spend some time in prayer. I hadn't prayed regularly in a while, but something inside me urged me to turn to prayer for solace. I went to a quiet corner of my home, away from the noise and distractions, and began to pray.

At first, my mind was still racing, filled with worries about the overwhelming workload and the discouraging atmosphere at work. But as I continued to pray, something remarkable happened. Slowly, I felt a sense of calm begin to wash over me. I poured out all my fears and anxieties to God, expressing my frustrations and seeking guidance. I asked for strength to handle the challenges and for peace to calm my troubled mind.

As I sat there in silence after my prayer, I felt a profound sense of peace that I hadn't felt in a long time. It was as if a heavy burden had been lifted from my shoulders. My mind, which had been clouded with stress and anxiety, was now clear and calm. I felt a renewed sense of strength and a quiet assurance that everything would be okay.

Over the next few weeks, I made it a point to take a few moments each day to pray. No matter how busy or chaotic my day was, I found time to retreat to that quiet corner and connect with the divine. This practice of daily prayer became my sanctuary, a sacred space where I could find peace amidst the storm.

The job remained challenging, especially with the high turnover rate and the indifferent management. The morale of my colleagues was still low, and the workload was heavy. But my perspective had shifted. I no longer felt overwhelmed by the pressure. Instead, I faced each day with a sense of calm and confidence, knowing that I was not alone in this journey. Prayer had become my anchor, grounding me and providing the inner peace I needed to navigate through the challenges.

Reflecting on that time, I realized how transformative the power of prayer can be. It taught me that no matter how chaotic life gets, there is always a place of peace and solace we can turn to. Prayer doesn't necessarily change our circumstances, but it changes our hearts and minds, giving us the strength and serenity to face whatever comes our way.

3. Spiritual Growth: Regular prayer fosters spiritual growth by encouraging self-reflection, humility, and a deeper understanding of one's faith. It helps individuals grow in their spiritual journey, becoming more attuned to their inner selves and the divine presence in their lives.

Example Prayer for Spiritual Growth
"Lord, help me to grow in my faith and understanding of your will. Open my heart to your teachings and guide me in your ways. Amen."

4. Guidance and Wisdom: Through prayer, individuals seek divine guidance and wisdom. It opens a channel for receiving insights, clarity, and direction in life's decisions and challenges.

Example Prayer for Guidance
"Heavenly Father, guide me with your wisdom and grace. Show me the path you have laid out for me, and grant me the strength to follow it with faith and courage. Amen."

5. Purpose and Meaning: Prayer can help individuals find a deeper sense of purpose and meaning in their lives. By reflecting on their beliefs and values, individuals can align their actions with their spiritual goals, creating a life that feels more fulfilling and purposeful.

Famous Quote: "The function of prayer is not to influence God, but rather to change the nature of the one who prays" (Søren Kierkegaard).

Emotional and Mental Benefits

The benefits of prayer extend beyond the spiritual realm, impacting emotional and mental well-being. Prayer can be a powerful tool for emotional healing and mental clarity:

1. Stress Reduction: Prayer has been shown to reduce stress and anxiety. By focusing on the divine and entrusting worries to a higher power, individuals can alleviate the burden of stress and find relief.

Famous Quote: "Do not be anxious about anything, but in every situation, by prayer and petition, with thanksgiving, present your requests to God" (Philippians 4:6).

2. Emotional Healing: Prayer can be a source of emotional healing, providing comfort and solace in times of grief, loss, or emotional pain. It allows individuals to express their feelings and find solace in the presence of a compassionate higher power.

   Example Prayer for Healing
   "Lord, I come to you with a heavy heart, seeking your healing touch. Mend my broken spirit, and fill me with your peace and love. Amen."

3. Mental Clarity: Engaging in prayer can enhance mental clarity and focus. It helps individuals clear their minds of distractions and gain a better understanding of their thoughts and emotions.

   Example Prayer for Mental Clarity
   "God, clear my mind of distractions and help me to focus on what truly matters. Grant me the clarity and insight to make wise decisions. Amen."

4. Resilience: Prayer fosters resilience by providing strength and support in the face of adversity. It helps individuals cope with life's challenges and maintain a positive outlook.

   Famous Quote: "God does not give us overcoming life; He gives us life as we overcome" (Oswald Chambers).

5. Emotional Regulation: Regular prayer can help individuals develop better emotional regulation. By turning to prayer during times of emotional turmoil, individuals can find a way to process their feelings and respond more calmly and thoughtfully.

Example Prayer for Emotional Regulation
"Lord, help me to manage my emotions and respond with grace and wisdom. Grant me the patience and strength to handle challenges with a calm heart. Amen."

Community and Unity

Prayer also plays a crucial role in fostering community and unity. It brings people together, creating a sense of belonging and shared purpose:

1. Building Community: Group prayer and communal worship foster a sense of community and belonging. It brings individuals together in shared faith and collective intention, strengthening social bonds.

   Famous Quote: "For where two or three gather in my name, there am I with them" (Matthew 18:20).

   Example of Communal Prayer
   "O God of all creation, we come together as one community, united in faith and purpose. Grant us the strength to support one another, the wisdom to act with compassion, and the courage to stand for justice. Amen."

2. Shared Purpose: Prayer unites individuals in a shared purpose, aligning their intentions and efforts toward common goals. Whether it is praying for peace, healing, or social justice, collective prayer amplifies the impact of individual efforts.

   Historical Event: During the civil rights movement, collective prayer played a significant role in uniting activists and providing them with strength and courage. Leaders like Martin Luther King Jr. often led prayers that inspired and motivated the movement.

3. Interfaith Dialogue: Prayer can also promote interfaith dialogue and understanding. By recognizing the commonalities in different prayer practices, individuals from diverse religious backgrounds can build bridges of mutual respect and cooperation.

   Example Prayer for Interfaith Unity
   "God of all nations, help us to see the common threads of love and compassion in our diverse faiths. Guide us to work together in harmony and understanding. Amen."

4. Support and Solidarity: In times of crisis or tragedy, communal prayer provides support and solidarity. It helps communities come together to offer comfort and aid to those in need.

   Famous Quote: "The highest form of worship is to find the least among you and treat them like Jesus" (Mother Teresa).

5. Strengthening Families: Prayer can also strengthen family bonds. When families pray together, it fosters a sense of unity, love, and mutual support, helping to build a strong and resilient family unit.

   Example Family Prayer
   "Heavenly Father, bless our family and keep us united in love and faith. Help us to support one another and grow together in your grace. Amen."

Transformational Power

The transformational power of prayer cannot be overstated.

It has the ability to change lives, alter circumstances, and bring about profound personal and societal transformation:

1. Personal Transformation: Prayer can lead to personal transformation by encouraging self-awareness, repentance, and a commitment to personal growth. It inspires individuals to align their lives with their spiritual values and principles.

   Famous Quote: "Prayer does not change God, but it changes him who prays" (Søren Kierkegaard).

   Example Prayer for Personal Transformation
   "Lord, transform my heart and mind. Help me to grow in your love and to become the person you created me to be. Amen."

2. Healing and Miracles: Throughout history, there have been numerous accounts of healing and miracles attributed to prayer. These stories highlight the extraordinary power of prayer to bring about physical, emotional, and spiritual healing.

   Historical Event: In 1858, Bernadette Soubirous reported visions of the Virgin Mary in Lourdes, France. The spring waters at the site of her visions have since been associated with miraculous healings, drawing millions of pilgrims each year.

   Example Miracle Prayer
   "Dear Lord, I believe in your power to heal and restore. I pray for your miraculous touch to heal my body, mind, and spirit. I trust in your divine plan. Amen."

3. Societal Change: Collective prayer movements have often been catalysts for social and political change. The power of prayer to mobilize and inspire action has been evident in various historical movements for justice and peace.

   Historical Event: The role of prayer in the abolitionist movement in the nineteenth century, where prayer meetings and vigils were integral in rallying support for the end of slavery, demonstrates its influence on societal transformation.

4. Renewed Hope: Prayer instills a sense of hope and optimism, even in the face of seemingly insurmountable challenges. It reminds individuals and communities of the possibility of positive change and the presence of a benevolent higher power.

Example Prayer for Hope
"God of hope, fill me with your light and love. When I feel overwhelmed, remind me of your promise that joy comes in the morning. Help me to hold onto hope and to trust in your divine plan. Amen."

5. Empowerment: Prayer can empower individuals and communities, giving them the strength and courage to stand up for justice, fight against oppression, and work toward a better world.

Famous Quote: "Faith is taking the first step even when you don't see the whole staircase" (Martin Luther King Jr.).

Example Prayer for Empowerment
"Lord, empower me with your strength and courage. Help me to stand up for what is right and to make a difference in the world. Amen."

6. Global Perspective: Prayer practices vary across cultures, yet they share a common goal of seeking divine connection and support. This universality of prayer highlights its importance in fostering a global sense of unity and compassion.

Story: In Japan, the Shinto practice of offering prayers at shrines involves writing wishes on small wooden plaques called ema and hanging them at the shrine. These prayers, ranging from personal hopes to global peace, show the deep cultural significance of prayer in Japanese society.

Example Shinto Prayer (Ema)

"Kami-sama, please watch over my family and bless us with health and happiness. Guide me in my studies and help me to achieve my dreams. Amen."

Reflection Questions

To help you further internalize the importance of prayer and apply the insights from this chapter to your own life, consider reflecting on the following questions:

1. Personal Connection
   - How do you currently connect with the divine through prayer? Are there specific types of prayer that resonate with you more than others?
   - Can you recall a time when prayer provided you with comfort, guidance, or strength? How did that experience impact your faith?

2. Spiritual Growth
   - In what ways has prayer contributed to your spiritual growth? Are there aspects of your prayer life that you would like to deepen or expand?
   - How can you incorporate more regular and meaningful prayer into your daily routine?

3. Emotional and Mental Well-Being
   - How does prayer help you manage stress and emotional challenges? Are there specific prayers or practices that you find particularly effective?
   - What role does prayer play in your mental clarity and focus? How can you use prayer to enhance your emotional regulation?

4. Community and Unity
   - How has communal prayer or group worship strengthened your sense of community and belonging? Are there ways you can become more involved in communal prayer activities?

- How can prayer help you foster better relationships within your family and community?

5. Transformational Impact
- Have you experienced personal transformation or witnessed societal change as a result of prayer? What lessons can you draw from these experiences?
- How can you use the power of prayer to inspire positive change in your life and in the world around you?

Conclusion

The importance of prayer extends far beyond its immediate spiritual benefits. It is a powerful tool for emotional and mental well-being, a unifying force within communities, and a catalyst for personal and societal transformation. By understanding and embracing the multifaceted importance of prayer, individuals can enrich their spiritual journeys and contribute to a more compassionate and connected world.

Prayer is a gift that transcends boundaries and unites humanity in its search for meaning, peace, and connection. As you continue your journey through this book, may you discover the profound impact that prayer can have on your life and the lives of those around you.

Prayer offers a path to inner peace, spiritual growth, and a deeper connection with the divine. It provides comfort in times of sorrow, guidance in moments of uncertainty, and strength in the face of adversity. Through prayer, individuals can find a sense of purpose, build stronger communities, and experience personal and societal transformation.

As you reflect on the importance of prayer, consider how it can enhance your own life and the lives of those around you. Embrace the practice of prayer with an open heart and mind, and allow it to lead you on a journey of spiritual discovery and growth. May you find solace, inspiration, and empowerment in your prayers, and may they bring you closer to the divine and to the true essence of your being.

Chapter 3

Developing a Prayer Practice

Creating a Sacred Space

Creating a sacred space for prayer is essential in fostering a deep and meaningful connection with the divine. A dedicated space can enhance your prayer experience by providing a tranquil environment where you can focus and reflect.

1. Choosing the Location
- Select a quiet and comfortable area in your home where you can pray without interruptions. This could be a corner of a room, a specific chair, or even a small nook.
- Consider the ambiance of the space. A location with natural light and a peaceful view can enhance the sense of tranquility.
- Think about outdoor spaces as well. A garden, balcony, or even a quiet spot in a nearby park can serve as a serene setting for prayer.

2. Personalizing Your Space
- Add items that inspire and uplift you, such as candles, incense, or essential oils. These can help create a calming atmosphere.

- Include symbols or objects that hold spiritual significance for you. This could be a cross, a prayer rug, a Buddha statue, or any other item that resonates with your faith.
- Incorporate comfortable seating, such as a cushion or chair, to ensure you can remain in a prayerful posture for extended periods without discomfort.
- Consider adding a small table or shelf to hold your prayer books, journals, and other spiritual items. Keeping these tools within easy reach can make your prayer time more focused and intentional.

3. Maintaining the Space
- Keep your sacred space clean and uncluttered. A tidy environment can help clear your mind and enhance your focus during prayer.
- Regularly refresh the space by changing the candles, flowers, or other items to keep it inviting and inspiring.
- Dedicate time each week to maintain and renew your sacred space. This practice itself can become a form of meditation and preparation for deeper prayer.

Establishing a Routine

Developing a consistent prayer routine can deepen your spiritual practice and make prayer a natural part of your daily life. Here are some steps to help you establish a regular prayer routine:

1. Setting a Schedule
- Identify the times of day when you can dedicate a few moments to prayer. This could be in the morning, during a lunch break, or before bed.
- Start with manageable increments of time, such as 5–10 minutes, and gradually increase the duration as you become more comfortable with your practice.
- Consider integrating prayer into your daily transitions, such as when you wake up, before meals, or as you end your day.

These natural pauses can serve as reminders to connect with the divine.

2. Creating a Ritual
- Develop a ritual that signals the beginning of your prayer time. This could be lighting a candle, taking a few deep breaths, or reading a short passage from a sacred text.
- Consistency in your ritual can help prepare your mind and body for prayer, making it easier to transition into a prayerful state.
- Customize your ritual to reflect your personal spiritual journey. For example, you might include a moment of gratitude, a short meditation, or a specific prayer posture that helps you feel more connected.

3. Incorporating Different Types of Prayer
- Vary your prayer practice by incorporating different types of prayer, such as supplication, thanksgiving, intercession, adoration, confession, meditation, and contemplation.
- This variety can keep your practice engaging and ensure that all aspects of your spiritual needs are addressed.
- Explore different prayer methods and traditions. For instance, you might try chanting, silent prayer, journaling, or using prayer beads. Each method can offer a unique way to connect with the divine.

4. Using Prayer Resources
- Utilize prayer books, apps, or online resources to find prayers that resonate with you and guide your practice.
- Join a prayer group or attend communal prayer services to gain support and inspiration from others.
- Seek out spiritual mentors or guides who can offer insights and encouragement as you develop your prayer routine.

Overcoming Challenges

Maintaining a consistent prayer practice can be challenging, especially in the face of busy schedules and distractions. Here are some common obstacles and strategies to overcome them:

1. Finding Time
-   Integrate prayer into your daily routine by associating it with regular activities. For example, you can pray during your morning commute while exercising or while performing household chores.
-   Set reminders on your phone or calendar to prompt you to take a break and pray.
-   Be flexible with your prayer times. If you miss a scheduled prayer session, find another moment in your day to reconnect. The key is consistency, not perfection.

2. Staying Focused
-   Begin your prayer time with a few moments of silence or deep breathing to clear your mind and center yourself.
-   If your mind wanders during prayer, gently redirect your focus back to your prayer or the presence of the divine.
-   Use visual aids, such as a candle flame or a sacred image, to help maintain your focus during prayer.

3. Dealing with Distractions
-   Choose a quiet time and place where you are less likely to be interrupted. Inform family members or housemates of your prayer times to minimize disruptions.
-   Use noise-canceling headphones or play soft instrumental music to block out external noise.
-   Embrace the practice of mindfulness during prayer. Acknowledge distractions without judgment and gently return your attention to your prayer.

4. Maintaining Motivation
- Reflect on the positive impact prayer has on your life and well-being. Keeping a prayer journal can help you track your experiences and recognize the benefits of your practice.
- Seek inspiration from spiritual readings, podcasts, or discussions with fellow practitioners to stay motivated and engaged.
- Celebrate milestones in your prayer journey, such as completing a month of consistent practice or experiencing a particularly meaningful prayer session.

Examples of Prayer Routines

To help you develop your own prayer routine, here are some examples of daily prayer practices:

1. Morning Prayer Routine
- Begin with a short meditation or breathing exercise to center yourself.
- Offer a prayer of thanksgiving for the new day and the opportunities it brings.
- Read a passage from a sacred text or a daily devotional.
- Conclude with a prayer for guidance and protection throughout the day.

  Example Morning Prayer
  "Good morning, Lord. Thank you for the gift of this new day. Guide me in your ways, protect me from harm, and help me to be a light to others. Amen."

2. Evening Prayer Routine
- Start by reflecting on the events of the day and expressing gratitude for the blessings you received.
- Offer a prayer of confession for any shortcomings or mistakes, seeking forgiveness and renewal.
- Pray for the well-being of loved ones and those in need.

-   End with a prayer for restful sleep and peace.

Example Evening Prayer
"Heavenly Father, thank you for the blessings of this day. Forgive me for any wrongs I have committed. Bless my loved ones and those in need. Grant me peaceful rest. Amen."

3. Midday Prayer Routine
-   Take a short break from your activities to reconnect with the divine.
-   Offer a prayer of supplication for any challenges you are facing.
-   Spend a few moments in silent meditation, focusing on the presence of the divine.
-   Conclude with a prayer of intercession for others who may be in need.

Example Midday Prayer
"Lord, I pause in the midst of this day to seek your guidance and strength. Help me with the challenges I face. May your presence be with those who are suffering. Amen."

Cultural Diversity in Prayer Practices

Prayer practices vary widely across cultures, yet they share the common goal of seeking divine connection and support. Here are some examples of prayer practices from different cultures and traditions:

1. Hinduism
    In Hinduism, prayer can take many forms, including chanting mantras, performing rituals (puja), and meditative practices. The use of prayer beads (mala) is common, with devotees reciting mantras as they count the beads.

    Example Prayer: "Om Namah Shivaya," a mantra dedicated to Lord Shiva, often chanted for protection and blessings.

2. Buddhism
   Buddhist prayer practices often involve chanting sutras or mantras, as well as meditation. The act of bowing before a Buddha statue and offering incense is also a common form of prayer.

   Example Prayer: "Namo Amituofo," a Pure Land Buddhist chant invoking the Buddha of Infinite Light and Life for spiritual guidance and salvation.

3. Islam
   Muslims perform Salah, the five daily prayers, facing the Kaaba in Mecca. These prayers include specific recitations and physical postures, such as bowing and prostration.

   Example Prayer: The Fajr prayer, performed before dawn, which includes verses from the Quran and supplications for guidance and mercy.

4. Native American Traditions
   Native American prayer practices often involve rituals and ceremonies that honor the natural world and ancestral spirits. The use of smudging with sage or sweetgrass, drumming, and dancing are integral to these practices.

   Example Prayer: A Lakota prayer of gratitude to the Great Spirit, often offered at sunrise to give thanks for the new day and its blessings.

5. Judaism
   Jewish prayer practices include reciting prayers from the Siddur (prayer book), such as the Shema and the Amidah. Observant Jews pray three times a day, incorporating blessings and psalms.

Example Prayer: The Shema, a declaration of faith in one God, recited twice daily: "Hear, O Israel: The Lord our God, the Lord is one."

6. Christianity
    Christian prayer practices vary by denomination but often include personal prayer, communal worship, and the recitation of traditional prayers like the Lord's Prayer.

    Example Prayer: The Lord's Prayer, taught by Jesus to his disciples: "Our Father, who art in heaven, hallowed be thy name. Thy kingdom come, thy will be done, on earth as it is in heaven. Give us this day our daily bread. And forgive us our trespasses, as we forgive those who trespasses against us. And lead us not into temptation; but deliver us from evil. For thine is the kingdom, the power and the glory, for ever and ever. Amen.

7. Shinto
    In Shinto, the indigenous faith of Japan, prayer practices include offering prayers at shrines, clapping hands to alert the kami (spirits), and making offerings of food and drink.

    Example Prayer: "Kami-sama, please watch over my family and bless us with health and happiness. Guide me in my studies and help me to achieve my dreams. Amen."

These diverse prayer practices highlight the universal nature of prayer and its importance across different cultures. By exploring and incorporating elements from various traditions, you can enrich your own prayer practice and deepen your spiritual journey.

Reflection Questions

To help you deepen your prayer practice, consider reflecting on the following questions:

1. Creating a Sacred Space
    - What elements would make your prayer space feel sacred and inviting? How can you personalize it to reflect your spiritual journey?

    - How does having a dedicated prayer space enhance your connection with the divine?

2. Establishing a Routine
    - What times of day are most conducive to prayer for you? How can you incorporate prayer into your daily routine?
    - What rituals or practices help you transition into a prayerful state?

3. Overcoming Challenges
    - What obstacles do you face in maintaining a consistent prayer practice? What strategies can you implement to overcome them?
    - How can you stay motivated and inspired in your prayer journey?

4. Personalizing Your Practice
    - How can you incorporate different types of prayer into your routine to address various spiritual needs?
    - What resources or community support can help you deepen your prayer practice?

5. Evaluating Progress
    - How has your prayer practice evolved over time? What changes have you noticed in your spiritual life as a result?
    - Are there any new prayer methods or practices you would like to explore?

Conclusion

Developing a prayer practice is a deeply personal and transformative journey. By creating a sacred space, establishing a consistent routine, and overcoming challenges, you can deepen your connection with the divine and enrich your spiritual life. Prayer is a powerful tool that offers solace, guidance, and strength, helping you navigate the complexities of life with grace and confidence.

As you continue to cultivate your prayer practice, may you find peace, inspiration, and a profound sense of connection with the divine. Embrace the journey with an open heart and mind, and allow prayer to guide you on your path to spiritual growth and fulfillment.

Prayer is not only a daily ritual but a journey that evolves with you. It adapts to your changing circumstances and grows with your spiritual maturity. As you deepen your practice, you will find that prayer becomes an integral part of your life, offering a source of unwavering strength and serenity.

May your prayer practice be a source of continuous growth, bringing you closer to the divine and to your true self. Embrace the journey with joy and dedication, knowing that each prayer is a step toward a deeper and more fulfilling spiritual life.

Chapter 4

Deepening Your Prayer Practice

Exploring Different Prayer Techniques

As you continue to develop your prayer practice, exploring various prayer techniques can enrich your spiritual experience and deepen your connection with the divine. Here are some diverse techniques to consider:

1. Lectio Divina
   Originating in Christian monastic traditions, Lectio Divina involves reading sacred texts in a meditative and contemplative manner.
   The practice consists of four steps: *lectio* (reading), *meditatio* (meditation), *oratio* (prayer), and *contemplatio* (contemplation). Choose a passage from a sacred text, read it slowly, and reflect on its deeper meaning. Allow the words to resonate within you and inspire your prayer.

   Example: If you select a passage from the Psalms, read it several times, each time focusing on different aspects and how they speak to your current situation.

2. Centering Prayer

Centering prayer is a method of silent prayer that prepares you to experience God's presence.

Sit comfortably with your eyes closed, and silently introduce a sacred word or phrase, such as *peace* or *love*, as a symbol of your intention to consent to God's presence.

When distractions arise, gently return your focus to the sacred word.

Example: Dedicate twenty minutes each morning to centering prayer, starting and ending with a brief reading from a devotional text.

3. Mantra Meditation

Common in Hindu and Buddhist traditions, mantra meditation involves repeating a sacred word or phrase to focus the mind and enter a state of deep meditation.

Choose a mantra that resonates with you, such as "om" or "Om Mani Padme Hum," and repeat it silently or aloud, allowing it to guide your meditation.

Example: Incorporate mantra meditation into your evening routine, using the practice to unwind and prepare for restful sleep.

4. The Examen

The Examen is a prayer technique from the Jesuit tradition, focusing on reviewing your day with gratitude and reflection.

Spend a few moments in silence, recalling the events of your day. Identify moments of gratitude, joy, and divine presence, as well as times of struggle or challenge.

Offer prayers of thanksgiving and seek guidance for areas where improvement is needed.

Example: Conclude your day with the Examen, writing down your reflections in a journal to track your spiritual growth over time.

5. Praying with Icons
    In Eastern Orthodox Christianity, icons are used as windows to the divine, aiding in contemplative prayer.
    Choose an icon that speaks to you, such as an image of Christ, the Virgin Mary, or a saint. Sit quietly and gaze at the icon, allowing it to draw you into deeper contemplation and prayer.

    Example: Set up a small icon corner in your home and spend 10–15 minutes each day in contemplative prayer before the icons.

Incorporating Movement in Prayer

Incorporating movement into your prayer practice can engage your body, mind, and spirit, creating a more holistic approach to prayer. Here are some ways to incorporate movement:

1. Walking Meditation
    Walking meditation involves mindfully walking while focusing on the sensations of each step and the rhythm of your breath. Choose a quiet, comfortable place to walk, and begin walking slowly. Pay attention to the movement of your body and the contact of your feet with the ground. Use this time to connect with the divine and reflect on your intentions.

    Example: Dedicate your lunch break to a fifteen-minute walking meditation in a nearby park, using this time to reconnect with your spiritual center.

2. Yoga
    Yoga combines physical postures, breath control, and meditation to create a spiritual practice that integrates body and mind.

Choose a style of yoga that resonates with you, such as Hatha, Vinyasa, or Kundalini. Incorporate prayers or affirmations into your practice, using each pose as an opportunity for contemplation and connection with the divine.

Example: Begin each morning with a thirty-minute yoga session, ending with a few minutes of meditation and a prayer of gratitude.

3. Dance
   Dance can be a powerful form of prayer, allowing you to express your emotions and connect with the divine through movement. Create a space where you can move freely, and choose music that inspires you. Allow your body to move intuitively, using dance as a form of expression and prayer.

   Example: Set aside time each week for a dance prayer session, using this practice to release stress and connect with the divine.

4. Tai Chi
   Tai Chi is a Chinese martial art that involves slow, flowing movements and deep breathing.
   Practice Tai Chi as a form of moving meditation, focusing on the flow of energy (qi) through your body and connecting with the divine presence within and around you.

   Example: Integrate a twenty-minute Tai Chi practice into your daily routine, using this time to center yourself and cultivate inner peace.

Combining Movement with Mantra Meditation

Combining movement with mantra meditation can enhance your prayer experience by engaging both the body and mind. This integrated approach can deepen your focus, create a sense of harmony, and foster a more profound connection with the divine.

1. Walking with a Mantra

   As you engage in walking meditation, incorporate the repetition of a mantra. With each step, silently repeat your chosen mantra, synchronizing the rhythm of your steps with the rhythm of the mantra.

   Example: Choose a quiet path for your walk. As you step with your right foot, silently say "om," and as you step with your left foot, repeat "shanti" (which means *peace*). Continue this rhythm, allowing the mantra to guide your pace and focus.

2. Yoga with Mantra

   Integrate mantra meditation into your yoga practice. Begin your session with a specific mantra and repeat it silently as you move through each pose. This can help maintain your focus and enhance the meditative quality of your practice.

   Example: Start your yoga session with the mantra "Om Namah Shivaya" (I bow to Shiva, the supreme God of transformation). As you transition between poses, silently repeat the mantra, allowing it to guide your breath and movements.

3. Tai Chi with Mantra

   Combine the slow, flowing movements of Tai Chi with the repetition of a mantra. This integration can help you stay centered and focused, enhancing the spiritual aspect of your practice.

   Example: As you perform Tai Chi movements, repeat the mantra "Om Mani Padme Hum" (the jewel is in the lotus) with each flow. Let the mantra guide your movements, creating a seamless connection between your body, mind, and spirit.

Using Art in Prayer

Art can be a powerful tool for deepening your prayer practice, allowing you to express your spirituality creatively. Here are some ways to incorporate art into your prayer:

1. Drawing and Painting
   Use drawing or painting as a form of prayerful expression. Allow your creativity to flow without judgment, creating images that reflect your inner spiritual journey.
   Focus on the process rather than the outcome, using art as a means of connecting with the divine and exploring your spirituality.

   Example: Dedicate a weekend afternoon to painting or drawing as a form of prayer, allowing the colors and shapes to express your prayers and emotions.

2. Journaling
   Prayer journaling involves writing down your prayers, reflections, and spiritual experiences.
   Set aside time each day to write in your journal, recording your thoughts, emotions, and insights. Use prompts or questions to guide your reflections, and allow your journal to be a space for honest and open communication with the divine.

   Example: Spend 10–15 minutes each evening journaling about your day's experiences and your conversations with the divine.

3. Mandalas
   Creating or coloring mandalas can be a meditative and prayerful practice. Mandalas are geometric designs that represent the universe and the divine.

Use mandala coloring books or create your own designs. As you work on the mandala, focus on your intentions and prayers, allowing the process to guide you into deeper contemplation.

Example: Incorporate mandala coloring into your weekly spiritual practice, using this time for reflection and prayer.

4. Collage
   Creating a collage can be a way to visually express your prayers and spiritual journey.
   Gather magazines, photographs, and other materials, and create a collage that represents your prayers, hopes, and dreams. Use this collage as a visual reminder of your spiritual intentions and aspirations.

   Example: Spend a quiet evening each month creating a new collage that reflects your current spiritual journey and goals.

Community Prayer Practices

Engaging in communal prayer can strengthen your sense of belonging and deepen your spiritual practice. Here are some ways to participate in community prayer:

1. Prayer Groups
   Joining a prayer group can provide support, encouragement, and accountability for your prayer practice.
   Find a local or online prayer group that resonates with your spiritual beliefs and practices. Participate regularly, sharing your prayers and experiences with others.

   Example: Join a weekly prayer group at your place of worship or online, committing to regular attendance and active participation.

2. Retreats:

Attending a spiritual retreat can offer an opportunity for intensive prayer, reflection, and renewal.

Look for retreats that align with your spiritual path, whether they focus on silent meditation, guided prayer, or communal worship. Use the retreat as a time to deepen your prayer practice and connect with like-minded individuals.

Example: Plan to attend an annual retreat that focuses on deepening your prayer practice, allowing you to step away from daily distractions and immerse yourself in spiritual growth.

3. Worship Services:

Participating in regular worship services can provide structure and community for your prayer life.

Find a faith community that aligns with your beliefs and values, and attend services regularly. Engage in the communal prayers, hymns, and rituals, allowing them to enrich your personal prayer practice.

Example: Make it a habit to attend weekly worship services, actively participating in the prayers and songs as a way to strengthen your connection with the divine and your community.

4. Interfaith Gatherings:

Engaging in interfaith prayer gatherings can broaden your understanding of different prayer practices and foster a sense of global spiritual unity.

Attend interfaith events, such as prayer breakfasts, vigils, or meditation sessions. Share your own prayer practices and learn from the diverse traditions represented.

Example: Participate in an interfaith prayer gathering in your community, using the opportunity to learn about and respect different spiritual traditions.

Personal Anecdote: Rediscovering Community through Prayer

A few years ago, I made the decision to relocate to a new area. It was an area I had lived in six years prior when I was serving in the military. Returning to this familiar yet changed environment was both exciting and daunting. Most of the friends and acquaintances I had known during my military days had moved away, leaving the city feeling somewhat unfamiliar and lonely.

Settling into my new job and routine, I found myself yearning for a sense of connection and community. Although the city had changed, my memories of it remained vivid, and I hoped to rekindle some of the camaraderie I once enjoyed. Despite my best efforts, establishing new relationships proved to be more challenging than I anticipated.

One day, out of the blue, an old high school friend who lived about forty-five minutes away reached out to me. We caught up on life, and during our conversation, she mentioned a prayer line phone call she joined every morning. She invited me to join, suggesting it might provide a sense of community and spiritual support during my transition.

Initially, I was hesitant. The idea of joining a group of strangers over the phone for prayer felt intimidating. However, my friend's encouragement and the desire for connection persuaded me to give it a try.

The first morning I dialed into the prayer line, I felt a mix of anxiety and curiosity. The call started with a brief introduction from the host, followed by each participant sharing their prayer requests. As I listened to the voices on the line, I realized that everyone was there for similar reasons—seeking support, connection, and spiritual growth.

The warmth and sincerity of the group's prayers created a powerful sense of community. Despite the physical distance, I felt an immediate sense of belonging. Over the next few weeks, joining the morning prayer line became a cherished part of my routine. Each call started with a devotional reading, followed by a time of shared prayer. The act of coming together, even virtually, to pray and support one another created a powerful sense of community. I found solace in knowing that others were praying for me and that I could offer my prayers and support in return.

Inspired by the prayer line, I decided to explore other ways to deepen my prayer practice and integrate more physical activity into my routine. I started attending gym classes after work, looking for a way to connect with others and relieve some of the stress from my new job. One evening, I signed up for a yoga class.

I had never tried yoga before, but I was open to the experience. The instructor led us through various poses, encouraging us to focus on our breath and be present in the moment. At the end of the class, we were introduced to a meditation exercise. As I sat there, focusing on my breath and letting go of the day's worries, I felt a profound sense of peace and clarity.

Intrigued by this new practice, I began incorporating meditation into my daily routine. Each evening, I dedicated a few minutes to sitting quietly, focusing on my breath, and reflecting on the day's events. This practice helped me unwind and prepare for restful sleep, bringing a new dimension to my prayer life.

The combination of the morning prayer line and my evening meditation practice had a transformative effect on my spiritual journey. The prayer line provided the community and spiritual support I desperately needed, helping me feel less alone and more grounded in my faith. The meditation classes introduced me to a new way of connecting with the divine, bringing a sense of calm and balance to my life.

Together, these practices inspired me to explore my spirituality more deeply. I realized that prayer and meditation could work hand-in-hand, each enriching the other. The support and connection from the prayer line, combined with the inner peace and clarity from meditation, helped me navigate my new environment with confidence and grace.

Reflecting on this journey, I learned that prayer is a powerful tool for building community and finding support, while meditation offers a path to inner peace and self-discovery. By integrating these practices into my daily life, I discovered a deeper connection with the divine and a greater sense of fulfillment and joy.

Reflection Questions

To help you deepen your prayer practice, consider reflecting on the following questions:

1. Exploring Techniques
    -   Which new prayer techniques resonate with you? How can you incorporate them into your existing practice?
    -   How does exploring different prayer techniques enrich your spiritual journey?

2. Incorporating Movement
    -   How can movement enhance your prayer experience? Which forms of movement resonate with your spiritual practice?
    -   How does incorporating movement into your prayer practice help you connect more deeply with the divine?

3. Using Art
    -   How can artistic expression be a form of prayer for you? Which artistic practices would you like to explore?
    -   How does using art in prayer help you express your spirituality and connect with the divine?

4. Community Prayer
    -   How can engaging in community prayer strengthen your spiritual practice? What opportunities for communal prayer are available to you?

- How does participating in communal prayer practices enhance your sense of belonging and support your spiritual growth?

5. Personalizing Your Practice
- How can you personalize your prayer practice to reflect your unique spiritual journey? What new elements would you like to incorporate?
- How does personalizing your prayer practice help you stay motivated and inspired?

Additional Resources for Deepening Your Prayer Practice

To further enrich your prayer practice, consider exploring the following resources:

1. Books
- *The Book of Common Prayer*—a compilation of traditional prayers used in Anglican worship.
- *The Way of a Pilgrim*—an anonymous Russian spiritual classic about the practice of the Jesus Prayer.
- *Praying with Icons* by Jim Forest—a guide to using icons in prayer.

2. Apps and Websites
- *Pray As You Go*: A daily prayer podcast designed to go with you wherever you are.
- Insight Timer: A meditation app with a variety of guided meditations and prayer resources.
- Sacred Space: An online prayer site run by the Irish Jesuits offering daily prayer and reflection.

3. Communities
- Join online forums or social media groups dedicated to prayer and spiritual growth.

- Seek out local prayer groups, meditation centers, or spiritual communities.

4. Workshops and Courses
- Attend workshops or courses on prayer techniques, meditation, or spiritual development offered by religious institutions or spiritual centers.
- Participate in webinars or online courses that focus on enhancing your prayer practice.

Conclusion

Deepening your prayer practice involves exploring new techniques, incorporating movement and art, and engaging in community prayer. By expanding your practice and embracing diverse methods, you can enrich your spiritual journey and deepen your connection with the divine. Prayer is a dynamic and evolving practice that adapts to your spiritual growth and changing circumstances.

As you continue to cultivate your prayer practice, may you find inspiration, creativity, and a profound sense of connection with the divine. Embrace the journey with an open heart and mind, allowing prayer to guide you on your path to spiritual growth and fulfillment.

Prayer is a journey that unfolds with each step you take. By exploring new methods, embracing creativity, and engaging with a community, you can create a rich and fulfilling prayer practice that sustains you throughout your spiritual journey.

May your prayer practice be a source of continuous growth, bringing you closer to the divine and to your true self. Embrace the journey with joy and dedication, knowing that each prayer is a step toward a deeper and more fulfilling spiritual life.

Chapter 5

Cultivating Inner Stillness

In the journey of prayer and spiritual growth, cultivating inner stillness through the practice of silence can deepen your connection with the divine and foster personal transformation. Silence offers a profound opportunity to listen, reflect, and encounter the sacred within and around you.

Exploring the Practice of Silence

1. The Power of Silence
    Silence is not merely the absence of noise but a deliberate choice to create space for introspection and communion with the divine. External silence, such as finding quiet environments in nature or sacred spaces, allows you to tune into the subtle rhythms of creation and the presence of the divine. Internal silence involves quieting the mind, letting go of distractions, and opening yourself to spiritual insights and guidance. Communal silence, experienced in group settings or during shared prayer, fosters a collective mindfulness and reverence, amplifying the spiritual energy of the group.

    Example: Spending an early morning in a tranquil forest, away from the bustling city, one may find solace in the quiet rustle of leaves and the gentle flow of a nearby stream. In this serene environment, you feel a deep connection to the natural world and a profound sense of peace, allowing yourself to center in prayer and meditation. The stillness enveloped you like a comforting blanket, offering a moment of respite from the demands of daily life and a chance to reconnect with your innermost thoughts and feelings.

2. Silence in Prayer

   Integrating periods of silence into your prayer practice can enhance your contemplative experience and deepen your spiritual communion. Silent prayer, where you sit in stillness and presence before the divine, enables you to offer your thoughts, emotions, and desires without the need for words. This form of prayer encourages receptivity to spiritual insights and fosters a deeper intimacy with God.

   Example: Each evening, I set aside quiet moments in my prayer corner. I surrender my worries and aspirations, opening my heart to divine guidance and comfort. This sacred silence allows me to listen attentively to the whispers of my soul and the gentle nudges of divine presence, fostering a sense of peace and renewal. Through silent prayer, I have discovered a profound connection with God that transcends language and intellect, embracing a communion of the spirit that nourishes my soul and brings clarity to my life's journey.

3. Listening in Silence

   Embracing silence as a practice of listening allows you to attune to your inner voice, the subtle promptings of the divine, and the needs of others. Cultivating a receptive spirit in moments of silence enables you to discern spiritual truths, gain clarity on life's complexities, and deepen your relationship with God.

   Example: During a silent retreat at a remote monastery, one can immersed themself in the stillness of the chapel's sacred space. With each breath, they can embrace the quietude and allow their heart to become a vessel for divine wisdom and compassion. In this profound silence, they can feel a deep communion with the divine presence and a renewed sense of purpose in my spiritual journey. Listening in silence has taught me the art of being present with God and others, where words are unnecessary and the language of the heart speaks volumes. It is in these moments of profound stillness that you have to learn to listen not only to the whispers of your own soul but also to the gentle guidance of the divine, shaping your understanding of faith and deepening your relationship with God.

Personal Anecdote

In moments when I feel misunderstood or mistreated by friends and family, I have found solace in the practice of seeking solitude and silence. There was a particular time when tensions were high among my circle of friends, and I felt increasingly isolated in my thoughts and emotions. Despite the bustling energy of social gatherings and the comfort of familiar faces, I yearned for a deeper connection with myself and a clearer perspective on the situation.

One evening, after a particularly challenging interaction, I excused myself from the group and retreated to a quiet corner of my home. Enveloped in the stillness of the night, I sought refuge in silence. With each breath, I allowed myself to release the weight of unspoken frustrations and unmet expectations. In the gentle embrace of solitude, I found the space to reflect on my feelings and unravel the complexities of the relationships that mattered deeply to me.

As I sat in quiet contemplation, I realized that solitude was not about withdrawing from others but about reconnecting with my innermost thoughts and emotions. It was in these moments of silent reflection that I gained clarity on my own needs and aspirations, separate from the expectations of those around me. Through the practice of seeking solitude, I learned to honor my feelings of vulnerability and uncertainty while nurturing a sense of resilience and self-awareness.

In the embrace of silence, I discovered a sanctuary where I could listen to the whispers of my heart and discern the path forward with clarity and conviction. This practice of separating myself from the noise of external expectations and finding refuge in silence has become an essential part of my journey toward self-discovery and emotional well-being.

Moreover, these moments of solitude helped me to fully gain clarity and recognize that true friendship is marked by unwavering support in every aspect. A genuine friend does not speak ill of you behind your back, mock you to others, or spread misinformation about you. Instead, they uplift and encourage you, celebrating your successes and offering a listening ear during challenging times. If ever there is negativity or condescension, it often stems from jealousy or underlying issues that the person may have, revealing their true intentions and prompting a reassessment of the relationship.

Embracing Solitude and Retreat

Solitude and retreat offer sacred spaces for introspection, renewal, and the deepening of your spiritual life. These intentional practices provide opportunities to withdraw from daily distractions, cultivate inner stillness, and nurture your relationship with the divine.

1. Solitude as Spiritual Practice:
   Creating intentional moments of solitude allows you to reconnect with your innermost thoughts, emotions, and spiritual aspirations. Solitude provides a sanctuary for prayer, reflection, and discernment, offering clarity and insight into life's challenges and blessings.

   Example: On a quiet afternoon, I retreated to a secluded corner of my home, away from the hustle and bustle of daily routines.

In this sacred solitude, surrounded by the comforting embrace of silence, I began a journey of self-discovery and spiritual renewal. Through prayer and contemplation, I uncovered hidden insights and embraced moments of grace, deepening my connection with the divine presence within and around me. Solitude has become my sanctuary, a sacred space where I can commune with God in quiet reflection, seeking wisdom and guidance for my spiritual journey.

2. Retreats for Spiritual Renewal

   Engaging in structured retreats tailored to spiritual growth and reflection provides dedicated time and space for deepening your prayer practice and spiritual understanding. Retreats offer guidance in prayer, meditation, and community fellowship, fostering a supportive environment for spiritual transformation.

   Example: Taking a weekend retreat at a serene retreat center, you can immersed yourself in a program of guided meditation, reflective journaling, and communal prayer. Surrounded by fellow seekers on the spiritual path, you discovered a sense of belonging and shared purpose. Together, everyone explored sacred teachings, embraced moments of silence, and nurtured our spiritual bonds, enriching our individual journeys of faith and renewal.

   Retreats have become pivotal moments of spiritual renewal for some, where they can retreat from the noise of the world and immerse themself in prayer and reflection, deepening their relationship with God and finding inspiration for their spiritual journey.

Practicing Mindfulness and Presence

Mindfulness cultivates a state of present-moment awareness, enabling you to deepen your connection with the divine and experience each moment more fully. By integrating mindfulness into your prayer life and daily activities, you can nurture a profound sense of gratitude, peace, and spiritual fulfillment.

1. Mindfulness in Prayer
   Incorporating mindfulness techniques, such as focused breathing and body awareness, enhances your prayer practice by grounding you in the present moment. Mindful prayer encourages attentiveness to God's presence, fostering a deeper communion and receptivity to divine guidance.

   Example: Before beginning your morning prayers, practice mindful breathing exercises to center yourself in the present moment. With each inhalation and exhalation, release tension and distractions, opening your heart to divine grace and inspiration. This mindful approach enriches your prayer experience, allowing you to offer heartfelt intentions and listen attentively to God's gentle whispers. Mindful prayer has transformed my spiritual practice, helping me to cultivate a deeper connection with God and fostering a sense of peace and clarity in my daily life.

2. Mindful Living
   Extending mindfulness beyond prayer into everyday activities, such as eating, walking, and listening, deepens your awareness and appreciation of life's sacred moments. Mindful living invites you to embrace each experience with gratitude and reverence, recognizing the divine presence in every encounter and interaction.

   Example: During a mindful walk in nature, I savor the beauty of blooming flowers and the soothing melody of birdsong. With each step, I practice mindful breathing, anchoring myself in the rhythm of nature and the divine presence surrounding me. This mindful awareness enriches my spiritual journey, fostering a deeper connection with God's creation and nurturing a sense of peace and harmony within. Mindful living has taught me to appreciate the sacredness of each moment, cultivating a spirit of gratitude and reverence for the divine presence that permeates all aspects of my life.

Reflection Questions

To deepen your exploration of inner stillness and mindfulness, consider reflecting on the following questions:

1. Silence and Prayer
- How does incorporating periods of silence enhance your prayer experience and deepen your spiritual communion?
- What insights or guidance have you received through silent prayer and contemplation?

2. Solitude and Retreat
- How can you create intentional spaces for solitude in your daily life, and what benefits do you experience from moments of sacred silence?
- In what ways have structured retreats supported your spiritual growth and renewal, and how do they deepen your connection with the divine?

3. Mindfulness and Presence
- How does practicing mindfulness in prayer enrich your experience of God's presence and deepen your spiritual journey?
- In what daily activities can you cultivate mindfulness to nurture a deeper sense of gratitude, peace, and spiritual fulfillment?

Conclusion

Cultivating inner stillness through silence, solitude, and mindfulness is a transformative journey that enriches your prayer practice and deepens your spiritual life. By embracing these sacred practices, you open yourself to profound encounters with the divine, gain clarity on life's complexities, and nurture a deeper sense of peace and purpose in your spiritual journey.

In the next chapter, we will explore the theme of gratitude and its role in spiritual growth and prayer. Stay tuned as we continue to expand and enrich your journey of prayer and spiritual discovery.

Chapter 6

Embracing Gratitude in Prayer

In the journey of prayer and spiritual growth, cultivating a spirit of gratitude can profoundly enrich your spiritual life and deepen your connection with the divine. Gratitude is not merely a polite gesture of thanks but a transformative practice that opens the heart, fosters humility, and enhances our awareness of blessings both big and small.

The Power of Gratitude

Gratitude is more than a simple expression of thanks; it is a state of being that radiates positivity and enriches our outlook on life. When we cultivate gratitude, we acknowledge the abundance of blessings, both big and small, that enrich our lives. This practice not only enhances our emotional well-being but also deepens our spiritual connection.

1. Understanding Gratitude
    Gratitude is a heartfelt acknowledgment of the gifts, blessings, and positive experiences in our lives. It shifts our focus from what we lack to what we have, fostering contentment and appreciation for the abundance that surrounds us. Cultivating gratitude involves recognizing the goodness in every moment, person, and circumstance, even amidst challenges and difficulties.

Example: Reflecting on ones journey, you may recall a time of financial struggle when a friend unexpectedly offered support without hesitation. In that moment, gratitude may welled up within you, transforming your anxiety into a profound sense of relief and appreciation for the kindness and generosity of others.

2. Gratitude in Prayer

   Integrating gratitude into your prayer practice enhances its depth and sincerity, allowing you to express thankfulness to the divine for blessings received and challenges overcome. Grateful prayer opens your heart to receive divine grace and guidance, fostering a deeper communion with God.

   Example: During my evening prayers, I set aside time to express gratitude for the day's blessings—moments of joy, lessons learned, and encounters that enriched my soul. This practice of grateful prayer helps me cultivate a positive mindset and deepen my faith in God's providence.

   Gratitude Prayer 1: A Prayer of Thanks and Praise

   Dear God,

   Today, I come before you with a heart full of gratitude. Thank you for the gift of life itself, for each breath that sustains me, and for the opportunity to experience your love and grace in my daily journey. I am grateful for the blessings that surround me—loving relationships, moments of joy and laughter, and the strength to face challenges with courage.

   Thank you for the beauty of creation—the majestic skies, the whispering trees, and the melodies of nature that uplift my spirit. May I always appreciate these wonders and find inspiration in their presence.

Help me, Lord, to cultivate a grateful heart, to see your hand at work in every aspect of my life, and to share your love with others through acts of kindness and compassion. Guide me to live each day with gratitude, knowing that in every moment, I am embraced by your infinite love.

In your holy name, Amen.

Gratitude Prayer 2: Blessings of Gratitude

Heavenly Father,

I humbly bow before you, overwhelmed by the abundance of blessings you have bestowed upon me. Thank you for the gift of family and friends who support and uplift me, for their love that mirrors your unconditional grace in my life.

I am grateful, Lord, for the challenges that have shaped me, for they have taught me resilience and deepened my faith in your divine plan. Thank you for the opportunities to grow, to learn, and to serve others in ways that honor your name.

Today, I offer you my heartfelt thanks for the simple pleasures of life—the warmth of the sun, the laughter of children, and the peace that comes from knowing you are always by my side. Help me to treasure these moments and to live with a spirit of gratitude that reflects your goodness to others.

May my life be a testament to your love and mercy, shining brightly as a beacon of hope and joy in a world that needs your light. I commit to living each day with a grateful heart, glorifying you in all that I do.

In your gracious name, Amen.

Embracing a Grateful Heart

1. The Transformative Power of Gratitude

   Embracing gratitude as a daily practice transforms our outlook on life, infusing each day with positivity and resilience. It shifts our perspective from scarcity to abundance, from complaint to appreciation, and from fear to trust in divine providence.

   Example: Through a deliberate practice of keeping a gratitude journal, I have experienced profound shifts in my attitude and emotional well-being. Recording three things I'm grateful for each day—whether simple joys, supportive relationships, or moments of personal growth—has cultivated a sense of inner peace and resilience, even during challenging times.

2. Gratitude and Spiritual Growth

   In the journey of spiritual growth, gratitude deepens our awareness of God's presence and blessings in our lives. It fosters humility and openness to divine guidance, nurturing a sense of reverence and awe for the mysteries of faith.

   Example: Participating in a gratitude retreat, I engaged in guided meditations and reflections that deepened my appreciation for the sacred gift of life. In moments of prayer and communal gratitude, I felt a profound sense of unity with others and a deepening connection with the divine presence that sustains and uplifts us all.

Practicing Gratitude in Daily Life

1. Mindful Gratitude Practices

   Integrating mindful gratitude practices into daily life enhances our ability to notice and appreciate the blessings that surround us. Mindfulness invites us to savor each moment, cultivating a deep sense of gratitude for the richness of life's experiences.

Example: During my morning walks and exercises, I practice mindful gratitude by noticing the beauty of nature—the warmth of the sun on my face, the song of birds, and the vibrant colors of flowers. Each step becomes a prayer of thankfulness, acknowledging the divine presence in the intricate tapestry of creation.

2. Gratitude and Relationships
    Expressing gratitude in our relationships strengthens bonds and fosters a spirit of generosity and compassion. Gratefulness cultivates empathy, kindness, and a willingness to support others, nurturing harmonious connections based on mutual respect and appreciation.

    Example: In a gesture of gratitude, I recently wrote heartfelt letters to friends and family, expressing my appreciation for their presence in my life. This act of gratitude deepened our relationships, fostering a sense of closeness and mutual support that transcends distance and time.

Examples of Expressing Gratitude

1. **Personal Thankfulness**
    - "Thank you for guiding me through moments of uncertainty and lighting my path with your wisdom."
    - "I am grateful for the love and support of my family, whose presence fills my life with warmth and joy."
    - "I appreciate the opportunity to learn from my mistakes and grow stronger each day."

2. **Gratitude for Opportunities**
    - "I am thankful for the chance to pursue my dreams and contribute positively to my community."
    - "Thank you for the challenges that have shaped me into the person I am today, resilient and determined."

- "I feel blessed to have the opportunity to make a meaningful impact through my work."

3. Appreciation in Relationships

- "I am grateful for the deep connections I share with friends who uplift me and share in both my joys and sorrows."
- "Thank you for the gift of true friendship, where I can be myself without fear of judgment."
- "I appreciate the kindness and compassion you show me, which inspires me to be a better person."

4. Gratitude for Health and Well-Being

- "I am thankful for the health and vitality that allow me to embrace each day with enthusiasm."
- "Thank you for the strength to overcome challenges and emerge stronger, both physically and emotionally."
- "I feel blessed to wake up each morning with a grateful heart, ready to embrace the gift of life."

5. Acknowledging Acts of Kindness

- "I am grateful for the generosity and support I have received during times of need."
- "Thank you for the small acts of kindness that brighten my day and remind me of the goodness in the world."
- "I appreciate your thoughtfulness and the effort you put into making a positive difference in my life."

6. Gratitude for Nature and Beauty

- "I am thankful for the beauty of nature and the peace it brings to my soul."
- "Thank you for the breathtaking sunrise that fills my heart with wonder."
- "I feel blessed to live in a world filled with such natural wonders."

7. Spiritual Gratitude

- "I am grateful for the guidance and wisdom that light my path."
- "Thank you for the blessings I receive each day, seen and unseen."
- "I appreciate the opportunity to grow spiritually and deepen my faith."

These examples illustrate various ways to express gratitude in everyday life, reflecting on blessings received, relationships cherished, and moments appreciated.

Reflection Questions

To deepen your exploration of gratitude in prayer and spiritual growth, consider reflecting on the following questions:

1. Gratitude in Prayer
   - How does practicing gratitude enhance your prayer experience and deepen your spiritual connection with God?
   - What are some meaningful moments of gratitude that have shaped your spiritual journey?

2. Daily Gratitude Practices
   - How can you incorporate mindful gratitude practices into your daily life to cultivate a deeper sense of appreciation and awareness?
   - What benefits have you experienced from keeping a gratitude journal or practicing gratitude rituals?

3. Gratitude and Relationships
   - How does expressing gratitude strengthen your relationships and nurture a spirit of generosity and compassion?
   - In what ways can you show gratitude to others in your community and beyond?

Conclusion

Embracing gratitude in prayer is a transformative practice that enriches your spiritual journey, deepens your connection with the divine, and enhances your overall well-being. By cultivating a grateful heart and integrating mindful gratitude practices into your daily life, you open yourself to the abundant blessings that surround you and nurture a spirit of joy, peace, and spiritual fulfillment.

In the next chapter, we will delve into the theme of resilience in prayer, exploring how resilience strengthens our faith and sustains us through life's challenges. Stay tuned as we continue to explore and enrich your journey of prayer and spiritual discovery.

Chapter 7

Nurturing Resilience through Prayer

In the journey of spiritual growth and personal development, resilience plays a crucial role in navigating life's challenges with grace and fortitude. Resilience enables us to withstand adversity, bounce back from setbacks, and emerge stronger in faith and character. Through the practice of prayer, we can nurture and cultivate resilience, drawing strength from our spiritual connection and deepening our trust in divine guidance.

Understanding Resilience

Resilience is the capacity to adapt and recover from difficulties, setbacks, and hardships. It involves cultivating inner strength, emotional flexibility, and a resilient mindset that enables us to face life's trials with courage and perseverance. Rather than being immune to stress or adversity, resilient individuals harness their spiritual resources to navigate challenges effectively and grow through adversity.

1. The Essence of Resilience
    Resilience is not about avoiding difficulties but about embracing them as opportunities for growth and spiritual maturation. It involves building emotional strength, maintaining hope, and finding meaning even in the midst of suffering. Resilient

individuals understand that life's challenges are not obstacles but stepping stones on the path to spiritual and personal growth.

Example: Reflecting on a difficult period in my life, I recall the loss of a loved one (my father). During this time, my faith and resilience were tested, but through prayer and seeking solace in the divine, I found the strength to carry on, honor their memory, and find meaning in the experience. This period of mourning became a time of profound spiritual growth, teaching me the importance of compassion, empathy, and the enduring power of love.

2. Resilience in Faith
    Resilience in faith involves trusting in God's plan, even when faced with uncertainty and hardship. It means believing that challenges have a purpose and that divine guidance will lead us through tough times. This trust in the divine nurtures a resilient spirit, allowing us to face life's trials with confidence and grace.

    Example: During a financial crisis, I turned to prayer, asking for strength and guidance. Through these prayers, I found not only practical solutions but also a renewed sense of hope and trust in God's provision. My faith became a source of strength, helping me navigate the crisis with a calm and steady heart, knowing that I was not alone.

Cultivating Resilience through Prayer

Prayer is a powerful tool for cultivating resilience. It provides a space to express our fears, seek guidance, and find peace. Through prayer, we connect with a higher power that offers support, wisdom, and strength.

1. Prayers for Strength and Guidance
    Praying for strength and guidance helps us tap into divine wisdom and find the courage to face challenges. These prayers

affirm our reliance on a higher power and reinforce our inner resolve.

Example: "Dear God, grant me the strength to face today's challenges with courage and grace. Guide me through my struggles and help me to find the wisdom and resilience to overcome them. Amen."

Through these prayers, we acknowledge our limitations and seek divine support, recognizing that true strength comes from our spiritual connection. This act of surrender and trust fosters resilience by reminding us that we are not alone in our struggles.

2. Prayers for Peace and Calm
    In times of turmoil, praying for peace and calm can help center our thoughts and emotions, allowing us to approach difficulties with a clear mind and a steady heart.

    Example: "Heavenly Father, in the midst of chaos, I seek your peace. Calm my anxious heart and fill me with your tranquility. Help me to trust in your plan and find solace in your presence. Amen."

    These prayers for peace create a sanctuary of calm within us, providing a refuge from the storm of life's challenges. They help us cultivate a resilient mindset by fostering inner peace and clarity, enabling us to respond to adversity with poise and confidence.

3. Prayers of Gratitude
    Expressing gratitude, even during challenging times, helps shift our focus from what is lacking to what is abundant. Gratitude in prayer fosters a positive mindset and reinforces our resilience.

    Example: "Lord, I thank you for the blessings in my life, even when they are hard to see. Help me to remain grateful for your love and guidance, and to find strength in your constant presence. Amen."

Gratitude prayers remind us of the goodness that still exists in our lives, even amidst adversity. They help us maintain a hopeful outlook and reinforce our resilience by cultivating a spirit of thankfulness and appreciation.

Embracing Challenges as Growth Opportunities

Adversity often brings valuable lessons and opportunities for growth. By embracing challenges and viewing them as opportunities for personal and spiritual development, we can enhance our resilience.

1. Learning from Adversity
   Challenges often teach us important life lessons and help us develop qualities, such as patience, compassion, and perseverance. By reflecting on these lessons in prayer, we can integrate them into our lives.

   Example: After someone losing a job, they will pray for understanding and guidance. Through this difficult period, they may learn the importance of adaptability and the value of seeking new opportunities. Their prayers will help them to see this setback as a chance for growth and reinvention.

   Embracing challenges as growth opportunities allows us to transform adversity into a catalyst for positive change. It encourages us to develop new skills, perspectives, and strengths, ultimately enhancing our resilience.

2. Finding Meaning in Suffering
   Finding meaning in suffering involves recognizing that pain and hardship can lead to profound spiritual growth. Through prayer, we can seek understanding and purpose in our struggles.

Example: A person who has a prolonged illness, will turned to prayer to find meaning and purpose in their suffering. Through their conversations with God, they will gain a deeper understanding of compassion and empathy, which will help enrich their relationships and spiritual life.

By finding meaning in suffering, we can transform our pain into a source of strength and wisdom. This perspective nurtures resilience by helping us see challenges as opportunities for growth and transformation.

Stories of Resilience from Faith Traditions

1. Biblical Examples of Resilience
    Throughout the Bible, numerous stories illustrate the resilience of individuals who faced great challenges but remained steadfast in their faith. These stories serve as powerful reminders of the strength that comes from relying on divine guidance.

    Example: The story of Job is a profound testament to resilience. Despite losing his wealth, health, and family, Job remained faithful to God. Through his suffering, he found strength and emerged with a deeper understanding of faith and trust in God's plan. Job's unwavering faith and resilience in the face of immense suffering inspire us to trust in divine wisdom and remain steadfast during our trials.

2. Saints and Spiritual Leaders
    Many saints and spiritual leaders have demonstrated remarkable resilience in their lives, often enduring persecution, hardship, and personal sacrifice. Their stories of resilience are sources of inspiration and guidance for us.

    Example: Saint Teresa of Ávila faced numerous challenges, including illness and opposition to her reform efforts. Despite these obstacles, her deep faith and commitment to prayer sustained her. Her writings on the interior life and the power of prayer continue to inspire and guide those seeking resilience and spiritual growth.

3. Modern Examples of Resilience
   In contemporary times, many individuals have exhibited extraordinary resilience through their faith. Their stories highlight the timeless nature of resilience and the power of prayer in overcoming adversity.

   Example: Nelson Mandela, although not solely a religious figure, often spoke of the strength he drew from his faith during his twenty-seven years of imprisonment. His resilience, forgiveness, and unwavering commitment to justice and reconciliation are profound examples of how faith can sustain and empower us through the darkest times.

Practical Steps to Cultivate Resilience

1. Daily Prayer Practice
   Establishing a daily prayer routine can be a cornerstone of resilience. Regular prayer provides a structured time to connect with the divine, reflect on our experiences, and seek guidance.

   Example: Set aside a specific time each day for prayer, whether in the morning to set a positive tone for the day or in the evening to reflect and give thanks. Consistency in prayer nurtures a resilient spirit by reinforcing our connection to a higher power.

2. Journaling with Prayer
   Combining journaling with prayer can be a powerful tool for resilience. Writing down prayers, reflections, and experiences helps process emotions and provides a record of growth and answered prayers.

Example: Keep a prayer journal where you write your thoughts, challenges, and prayers. Reflect on past entries to see how you've grown and how prayers have been answered, reinforcing your resilience and faith.

3. Meditative Prayer
Meditative prayer involves quieting the mind and focusing on a single thought, scripture, or aspect of the divine. This practice can enhance inner peace and resilience.

Example: Spend a few minutes each day in meditative prayer, focusing on a verse, such as "Be still, and know that I am God" (Psalm 46:10). This quiet time fosters a deep sense of peace and strengthens your resilience by grounding you in divine presence.

4. Community Support
Engaging with a faith community provides additional support and encouragement. Shared prayer, communal worship, and spiritual fellowship bolster resilience by reminding us that we are not alone.

Example: Join a prayer group or participate in communal worship services. Sharing your journey with others and supporting each other through prayer creates a strong network of resilience and faith.

Reflection Questions

1. Personal Resilience
- What specific experiences have tested your resilience, and how did prayer help you navigate those challenges?
- How can you develop a more consistent prayer practice to strengthen your resilience?

2. Spiritual Growth
- In what ways have you grown spiritually as a result of facing and overcoming challenges?
- How can you incorporate the lessons learned from adversity into your daily spiritual practices?

3. Community and Support
- How has your faith community supported you in times of difficulty, and how can you contribute to building resilience within your community?
- What steps can you take to foster a supportive and resilient faith community?

Conclusion

Nurturing resilience through prayer is a powerful practice that strengthens our faith and equips us to navigate life's challenges with grace and fortitude. By turning to prayer for strength, guidance, and peace, we tap into a divine source of support that enhances our resilience and enriches our spiritual journey. Through gratitude and embracing challenges as opportunities for growth, we develop a resilient spirit that can withstand life's storms and emerge stronger.

In the next chapter, we will explore the role of community in prayer and how shared spiritual practices can foster connection, support, and collective resilience. Stay tuned as we continue to explore and enrich your journey of prayer and spiritual discovery.

Chapter 8

The Role of Community in Prayer

Prayer is often seen as a deeply personal practice, a moment of solitude and connection with the divine. However, the power of communal prayer should not be underestimated. Gathering together in prayer strengthens bonds, fosters mutual support, and creates a shared spiritual energy that can uplift and inspire all members of the community. "To gather with God's people in united adoration of the Father is as necessary to the Christian life as prayer" (Pope John Paul II). In this chapter, we will explore the significance of communal prayer, the various ways it can be practiced, and the profound impact it can have on individuals and the community as a whole.

The Importance of Community in Prayer

1. Strengthening Bonds
    Communal prayer brings people together, fostering a sense of unity and belonging. It strengthens the bonds among community members, creating a supportive network that enhances each person's spiritual journey.

    Example: Weekly prayer meetings at a local church provide a space for congregants to share their joys and sorrows, pray for one another, and feel connected through their shared faith.

These gatherings foster a sense of family and mutual support that extends beyond the walls of the church. For instance, during these meetings, members often share personal stories and testimonies that help others understand and relate to their experiences. This deep sharing builds empathy and trust, creating an environment where everyone feels valued and supported.

2. Mutual Support
   In times of difficulty, communal prayer offers a powerful source of support and encouragement. Knowing that others are praying for you can provide immense comfort and strength.

   Example: During a family crisis, members of a prayer group gathered to offer prayers of support and encouragement. Their collective prayers provided a sense of peace and hope, helping the family navigate their challenges with a renewed sense of faith and resilience. When the family shared their struggles with the group, they were met with compassion and understanding. Each prayer offered by the group members reinforced the family's belief that they were not alone and that the divine was present in their ordeal, providing strength and guidance.

3. Shared Spiritual Energy
   Praying together creates a collective spiritual energy that can be profoundly uplifting. This shared energy can enhance the prayer experience, making it more powerful and impactful.

   Example: During a community prayer vigil, the collective energy of the participants created a palpable sense of peace and reverence. The shared experience of prayer deepened each participant's connection to the divine and to one another. For example, as candles were lit and prayers were spoken in unison, the atmosphere became charged with a tangible sense of unity and spiritual presence. Participants often reported feeling a deeper sense of calm and clarity, inspired by the collective faith and devotion surrounding them.

Biblical Foundation for Communal Prayer

The significance of communal prayer is highlighted in the Bible. In Matthew 18:20, Jesus says, "For where two or three gather in my name, there am I with them." This verse underscores the importance of gathering together in prayer and the divine presence that accompanies such gatherings. This biblical assurance offers comfort and reinforces the idea that communal prayer is not just a tradition but a spiritually enriching practice that invites divine presence and blessings.

Ways to Practice Communal Prayer

1. Prayer Groups
   Joining a prayer group provides a regular opportunity to pray with others, share prayer requests, and offer support. Prayer groups can meet in person or virtually, making them accessible to a wide range of participants.

   Example: A weekly virtual prayer group allows members from different parts of the world to come together in prayer. Despite the physical distance, the group members feel a deep sense of connection and support through their shared prayers. For example, during these virtual meetings, participants often share their prayer requests, offer words of encouragement, and follow up on previous prayer topics, fostering a sense of continuous support and interconnectedness that transcends geographical boundaries.

2. Worship Services
   Communal worship services, such as church services, offer a structured setting for communal prayer. These services often

include collective prayers, hymns, and rituals that enhance the communal prayer experience.

Example: Sunday morning worship services provide an opportunity for congregants to participate in collective prayers, sing hymns of praise, and engage in rituals that strengthen their faith and sense of community. For instance, the act of singing hymns together not only enhances the prayer experience but also fosters a sense of unity and shared purpose among the congregation. The recitation of creeds and communal responses during the service further solidifies the bond among participants, creating a strong sense of collective worship.

3. Prayer Vigils
   Prayer vigils are special gatherings focused on collective prayer and reflection. They are often held in response to specific events or needs and can be a powerful way to unite the community in prayer.

   Example: In response to a natural disaster, a community organized a prayer vigil to pray for those affected. The vigil provided a space for collective mourning, support, and a shared commitment to help those in need. For example, during the vigil, participants shared stories of those affected by the disaster, lit candles in their memory, and offered prayers for healing and recovery. This collective act of compassion and solidarity not only provided comfort to those directly impacted but also strengthened the community's resolve to support and assist in the recovery efforts.

4. Retreats and Workshops
   Spiritual retreats and prayer workshops offer extended opportunities for communal prayer and spiritual growth. These events provide a focused environment for participants to deepen their prayer practice and strengthen their spiritual connections.

Example: A weekend prayer retreat offered workshops on different prayer techniques, communal prayer sessions, and time for personal reflection. Participants left the retreat feeling spiritually rejuvenated and more connected to their faith community. During the retreat, participants engaged in various activities such as guided meditations, group discussions, and silent reflection periods. These activities allowed them to explore different aspects of their faith, gain new insights into their spiritual journey, and build deeper connections with fellow individuals at the retreat through shared experiences and mutual support.

The Impact of Communal Prayer on Individuals and the Community

1. Enhanced Spiritual Growth
   Participating in communal prayer can enhance individual spiritual growth by providing opportunities for learning, reflection, and shared experiences. It allows individuals to benefit from the collective wisdom and support of the community.

   Example: Through regular participation in a prayer group, individuals learn new prayer techniques, gain insights from others' experiences, and deepen their own spiritual practices. For instance, members may share personal stories of how specific prayers have impacted their lives, offering practical examples and inspiration that enrich the prayer experiences of others. This exchange of ideas and experiences fosters a deeper understanding and appreciation of different prayer practices, enhancing individual spiritual growth.

2. Emotional and Psychological Benefits
   Communal prayer can provide significant emotional and psychological benefits, including reduced stress, increased feelings of support, and a greater sense of peace and well-being.

Example: Members of a communal prayer group report feeling less isolated and more supported in their daily lives. The emotional and psychological support they receive from the group helps them cope with personal challenges more effectively. For example, during times of personal crisis or stress, group members often rally around the affected individual, offering prayers, words of encouragement, and practical support. This collective care and concern create a strong sense of community and belonging, which significantly enhances emotional and psychological well-being.

3. Strengthening Community Ties
    Communal prayer fosters a sense of unity and solidarity within the community. It strengthens relationships, builds trust, and encourages collective action toward common goals.

    Example: A community that regularly comes together in prayer is more likely to work together on service projects, support local initiatives, and respond collectively to community needs. For instance, a prayer group may decide to volunteer at a local food bank, organize fundraisers for community causes, or support each other in times of need. These collective actions, inspired by their prayer meetings, help build a stronger, more cohesive community that is united in purpose and action.

4. Creating a Culture of Compassion
    Engaging in communal prayer can cultivate a culture of compassion and empathy within the community. It encourages individuals to look beyond their own needs and consider the well-being of others.

    Example: A prayer group that regularly prays for the needs of the wider community is more likely to engage in acts of service and support for those in need. Their prayers inspire actions that reflect their commitment to compassion and kindness.

For instance, the group may organize drives to collect food, clothing, or other essentials for those in need. These acts of kindness and service, motivated by their collective prayers, help create a culture of empathy and compassion that extends beyond the group and impacts the wider community.

Reflection Questions

To deepen your exploration of the role of community in prayer, consider reflecting on the following questions:

1. Community and Connection
- How has participating in communal prayer strengthened your sense of connection to your faith community?
- What benefits have you experienced from praying with others?

2. Support and Encouragement
- How can you offer support and encouragement to others through communal prayer?
- In what ways can communal prayer provide comfort and strength during times of difficulty?

3. Collective Spiritual Energy
- How does the collective spiritual energy of communal prayer enhance your own prayer experience?
- What steps can you take to foster a sense of shared spiritual energy within your community?

Conclusion

The role of community in prayer is a powerful and transformative aspect of spiritual life. By coming together in prayer, we strengthen our bonds, offer mutual support, and create a shared spiritual energy that uplifts and inspires. Whether through prayer groups, worship services, prayer vigils, or retreats, communal prayer enriches our spiritual journey and fosters a deep sense of connection and unity within the community.

In the next chapter, we will explore the theme of forgiveness in prayer, examining how forgiveness can heal our hearts and deepen our relationship with the divine. Stay tuned as we continue to explore and enrich your journey of prayer and spiritual discovery.

Chapter 9

The Power of Forgiveness in Prayer

Forgiveness is a profound spiritual act that holds the power to heal, transform, and liberate. In the journey of prayer and spiritual growth, embracing forgiveness is essential for nurturing inner peace and deepening our relationship with the divine. This chapter explores the significance of forgiveness in prayer, the steps to cultivate a forgiving heart, and the transformative impact it can have on our lives.

Understanding Forgiveness

Forgiveness is the intentional and voluntary process of releasing feelings of resentment or vengeance toward someone who has wronged us. It is not about condoning harmful behavior or forgetting the past but about freeing ourselves from the emotional burden of anger and bitterness. Forgiveness is an act of grace that opens the heart to healing and reconciliation.

1. The Essence of Forgiveness
   Forgiveness involves letting go of negative emotions and choosing compassion over anger. It is a powerful way to reclaim inner peace and break free from the cycle of hurt.

Example: When a close friend betrayed my trust, I was overwhelmed with confusion and sadness. Through prayer and reflection, I sought the strength to forgive. By releasing any resentment, I found a renewed sense of peace and the ability to move forward without the weight of past grievances.

2. Forgiveness and Spiritual Growth
   Embracing forgiveness is a vital aspect of spiritual growth. It deepens our connection with the divine and aligns us with the principles of love and compassion.

   Example: In the Lord's Prayer, Jesus teaches us to pray, "Forgive us our trespasses, as we forgive those who trespass against us." This prayer highlights the reciprocal nature of forgiveness and its importance in our relationship with God.

Steps to Cultivate Forgiveness through Prayer

Cultivating forgiveness can be challenging, but incorporating specific practices into your prayer life can facilitate the process.

1. Prayer for Strength and Guidance
   Seeking divine assistance in the process of forgiveness is crucial. Prayers for strength and guidance can help us navigate the challenging emotions associated with forgiveness.

   Example: "Dear God, grant me the strength to forgive those who have wronged me. Guide my heart toward compassion and help me release the burden of anger and resentment. Amen."

2. Prayer for Healing
   Forgiveness is closely linked to healing. Praying for emotional and spiritual healing can facilitate the forgiveness process.

Example: "Heavenly Father, heal the wounds in my heart caused by past hurts. Help me to forgive and let go so that I may find peace and renewal in your love. Amen."

3. Reflective Prayer and Meditation
   Engaging in reflective prayer and meditation allows us to explore our feelings and gain insight into the reasons behind our pain. This introspection can foster a deeper understanding of the need for forgiveness.

   Example: During a quiet moment of meditation, reflect on the people or situations that have caused hurt. Ask for divine guidance to understand the root of your pain and the courage to forgive.

4. Gratitude and Forgiveness
   Practicing gratitude can shift our focus from hurt to healing. Prayers of gratitude can help us appreciate the positive aspects of our lives and cultivate a forgiving heart.

   Example: "Lord, I thank you for the blessings in my life. Help me to focus on your love and grace, and to extend forgiveness to others as an act of gratitude for your endless mercy. Amen."

Continuous Practice of Forgiveness

Forgiveness is not a one-time event but a continuous practice that requires dedication and persistence. Embracing forgiveness as an ongoing process allows us to maintain inner peace and spiritual growth.

1. Daily Reflection
   Make forgiveness a part of your daily reflection. Regularly examine your heart for any lingering resentment or unresolved conflicts and bring them to prayer.

Example: At the end of each day, spend a few moments in quiet reflection, asking yourself if there is anyone you need to forgive or seek forgiveness from. Offer these intentions in prayer, asking for strength and guidance to address them.

2. Forgiveness Rituals
   Incorporate forgiveness rituals into your spiritual practice. These rituals can serve as reminders of your commitment to living with a forgiving heart.

   Example: Create a simple ritual, such as lighting a candle and saying a prayer of forgiveness, whenever you feel burdened by resentment. This act can symbolize the release of negative emotions and the embrace of compassion.

3. Community Support
   Engage with a faith community that values and practices forgiveness. Being part of a supportive community can reinforce your commitment to forgiveness and provide encouragement during challenging times.

   Example: Join a prayer group or attend worship services that emphasize forgiveness and reconciliation. Sharing your journey with others can provide valuable support and inspiration.

Biblical Verses on Forgiveness

The Bible offers numerous teachings on the importance of forgiveness, providing wisdom and guidance for those seeking to cultivate a forgiving heart.

1. Ephesians 4:32
   "Be kind and compassionate to one another, forgiving each other, just as in Christ God forgave you."

This verse emphasizes the need for kindness and compassion, reminding us that our forgiveness of others should mirror the forgiveness we have received from God.

2. Colossians 3:13
"Bear with each other and forgive one another if any of you has a grievance against someone. Forgive as the Lord forgave you."

Here, the apostle Paul encourages believers to bear with one another and to forgive, reflecting the divine forgiveness they have experienced.

3. Matthew 6:14–15
"For if you forgive other people when they sin against you, your heavenly Father will also forgive you. But if you do not forgive others their sins, your Father will not forgive your sins."

Jesus teaches the conditional nature of forgiveness, stressing that our own forgiveness is tied to our willingness to forgive others.

Famous Quotes on Forgiveness

In addition to biblical teachings, many influential figures have spoken about the power of forgiveness. Their words can inspire and guide us in our journey of forgiveness.

1. Martin Luther King Jr.
"Forgiveness is not an occasional act; it is a constant attitude."

This quote highlights the importance of making forgiveness a consistent part of our lives, rather than a one-time gesture.

2. Mahatma Gandhi
"The weak can never forgive. Forgiveness is the attribute of the strong."

Gandhi's words remind us that forgiveness requires strength and courage, and it is a mark of inner strength rather than weakness.

3. Lewis B. Smedes
"To forgive is to set a prisoner free and discover that the prisoner was you."

This quote captures the liberating power of forgiveness, emphasizing that forgiving others ultimately frees ourselves.

The Importance of Forgiving Yourself

Forgiving others is vital, but equally important is the act of forgiving oneself. Self-forgiveness is crucial for personal healing and spiritual growth.

1. Releasing Self-Judgment
Forgiving oneself involves letting go of self-judgment and guilt. It is about accepting our imperfections and learning from our mistakes.

Example: After an argument with a loved one, I was consumed with guilt over the harsh words I had spoken. Through prayer and self-reflection, I sought forgiveness for myself, recognizing that everyone has moments of weakness. This self-forgiveness allowed me to apologize sincerely and rebuild the relationship with greater empathy and understanding.

2. Self-Forgiveness and Healing
Self-forgiveness is a critical component of healing. It frees us from the chains of past mistakes and enables us to embrace a future filled with hope and possibility.

Example: "Dear God, help me to forgive myself for the mistakes I have made. Grant me the grace to learn from my errors and

the courage to move forward with a renewed sense of purpose.
Amen."

3. Embracing Self-Compassion
    Cultivating self-compassion is essential for self-forgiveness.
    It involves treating ourselves with the same kindness and
    understanding that we would offer to others.

    Example: Reflect on a past mistake and speak to yourself with
    compassion: "I am human, and I make mistakes. I forgive
    myself and choose to grow from this experience."

Exploring Challenges in Forgiveness

Forgiving others, and ourselves, is often fraught with challenges.
Understanding these obstacles can help us navigate the forgiveness
journey with greater resilience and compassion.

1. Deep-Seated Hurt
    Forgiving deep-seated hurt can be particularly challenging,
    especially when the pain is fresh or the wound is severe.

    Example: A betrayal by a close friend may leave lasting scars.
    In such cases, forgiveness may require time and ongoing effort.
    Prayer and spiritual guidance can provide the strength needed
    to begin on this journey.

2. Ongoing Conflict
    When we are in the midst of ongoing conflict, forgiveness can
    seem impossible. It is essential to seek divine assistance and
    practice patience.

    Example: In a difficult relationship with a family member,
    continuous disagreements can make forgiveness seem out of
    reach. Praying for patience and understanding, while setting

healthy boundaries, can help maintain a forgiving attitude even amid conflict.

3. Self-Blame and Guilt
   Self-forgiveness is often hindered by deep-seated guilt and self-blame. Overcoming these feelings requires compassion and self-acceptance.

   Example: After making a significant mistake, feelings of guilt can be overwhelming. Through prayer, reflection, and self-compassion, we can begin to release self-blame and embrace forgiveness.

4. Fear of Vulnerability
   Sometimes, forgiving someone may lead to the fear of reconciling and re-entering a potentially harmful relationship. Forgiveness does not always mean reconciliation; it can mean finding peace while maintaining healthy boundaries.

   Example: In cases of abuse or toxic relationships, forgiveness can be about finding inner peace and releasing anger without necessarily restoring the relationship. Praying for wisdom and strength can help navigate this complex dynamic.

Overcoming Challenges in Forgiveness

Forgiveness can be challenging, especially when dealing with deep-seated hurt or ongoing conflict. Recognizing and addressing these challenges can help us navigate the path to forgiveness more effectively.

1. Acknowledging Pain
   Forgiveness does not mean ignoring or minimizing the pain we have experienced. Acknowledging the hurt is an important step in the healing process.

Example: Allow yourself to feel and express the pain caused by someone's actions. Journaling, speaking with a trusted friend, or praying about your feelings can help you process the hurt and begin the journey toward forgiveness.

2. Setting Boundaries
Forgiving someone does not necessarily mean allowing them back into your life in the same way. Setting healthy boundaries can protect your well-being while still offering forgiveness.

Example: After forgiving a friend who repeatedly betrayed your trust, you may choose to redefine the relationship with clear boundaries to prevent further hurt while maintaining a spirit of forgiveness.

3. Seeking Support
Forgiving deep hurts can be difficult to do alone. Seeking support from trusted friends, faith leaders, or counselors can provide valuable guidance and encouragement.

Example: If you are struggling to forgive someone, consider seeking advice and support from a spiritual mentor or joining a support group focused on forgiveness and healing.

4. Practicing Patience
Forgiveness is often a gradual process that takes time. Being patient with yourself and the process is crucial.

Example: Understand that forgiveness may take time and effort. Pray for patience and perseverance as you work through your emotions and move toward a forgiving heart.

The Transformative Impact of Forgiveness

1. Inner Peace and Freedom

Forgiveness brings inner peace and emotional freedom. By letting go of grudges, we free ourselves from the negative impact of past hurts.

Example: After forgiving a family member for a long-standing dispute, I felt a profound sense of relief and liberation. The burden of resentment lifted, allowing me to experience deeper peace and joy.

2. Healing Relationships
    Forgiveness can heal and restore relationships. It paves the way for reconciliation and renewed connections.

    Example: A strained relationship with a friend was transformed after we both sought forgiveness through prayer. Our willingness to forgive and be forgiven healed our bond and strengthened our friendship.

3. Spiritual Renewal
    Forgiveness is a path to spiritual renewal. It aligns us with divine principles and fosters a closer relationship with God.

    Example: Embracing forgiveness in prayer deepened my spiritual practice. I felt a renewed sense of God's presence and guidance in my life, knowing that I was living in accordance with divine love and compassion.

Reflection Questions

To deepen your exploration of forgiveness in prayer, consider reflecting on the following questions:

1. Personal Forgiveness
    -   What past hurts or grievances are you holding onto, and how can prayer help you release them?

- How has the act of forgiving someone positively impacted your life and spiritual growth?

2. Seeking Forgiveness
- In what ways can you seek forgiveness from those you may have wronged?
- How can prayer support you in the process of seeking and granting forgiveness?

3. Forgiving Yourself
- What mistakes or regrets are you holding against yourself, and how can you begin the process of self-forgiveness?
- How does self-compassion play a role in your journey of self-forgiveness?

4. Living with a Forgiving Heart
- How can you cultivate a forgiving heart in your daily interactions?
- What role does gratitude play in fostering forgiveness and compassion?

Conclusion

The power of forgiveness in prayer is transformative and liberating. By embracing forgiveness, we open our hearts to healing, restore relationships, and deepen our connection with the divine. Through prayer, we seek the strength and guidance to forgive, allowing us to live with greater peace, compassion, and spiritual fulfillment.

In the final chapter, we will reflect on the overall journey of prayer, summarizing the key themes explored and offering insights for continuing to deepen your spiritual practice. Stay tuned as we conclude our exploration of prayer and spiritual discovery.

Conclusion: Journey of the Heart

As we reach the conclusion of our exploration into the profound realms of prayer, it is essential to reflect on the transformative journey we have undertaken together. Throughout this book, we have delved into various aspects of prayer, from developing a practice and understanding its importance to deepening our spiritual connection through gratitude, resilience, and forgiveness.

Prayer is more than a ritual or a series of words; it is a living, dynamic relationship with the divine. It is through prayer that we find solace, guidance, and strength. We have discovered that prayer is not a solitary endeavor but a communal experience that unites us with others and amplifies our spiritual energy.

Key Themes and Insights

1. Understanding Prayer
   We began our journey by understanding the essence of prayer and its significance in our spiritual lives. Prayer is a bridge that connects us to the divine, allowing us to communicate, seek guidance, and express our deepest emotions.

2. Developing a Prayer Practice
   Establishing a consistent prayer practice is foundational to spiritual growth. Whether through silent meditation, spoken words, or communal worship, regular prayer nourishes our souls and strengthens our faith.

3. Embracing Gratitude
   Gratitude in prayer shifts our focus from what we lack to the abundance of blessings in our lives. By cultivating a grateful heart, we open ourselves to deeper spiritual fulfillment and a more profound connection with the divine.

4. Cultivating Resilience
   Prayer provides the strength to navigate life's challenges and uncertainties. Embracing resilience through prayer helps us overcome adversity, find hope in difficult times, and grow stronger in our faith.

5. The Power of Community
   Communal prayer fosters a sense of unity and belonging. It strengthens bonds, provides mutual support, and creates a shared spiritual energy that uplifts and inspires us.

6. The Journey of Forgiveness

Forgiveness is a transformative act that liberates us from the burdens of resentment and anger. Through prayer, we seek the strength to forgive others and ourselves, paving the way for healing, reconciliation, and spiritual renewal.

Embracing the Continuous Journey

Our journey of prayer and spiritual growth is ongoing. It is a continuous process that requires dedication, reflection, and openness to divine guidance. As we move forward, let us remember that each moment of prayer is an opportunity to deepen our relationship with the divine and to cultivate a heart filled with love, compassion, and forgiveness.

Final Reflection Questions

As you continue your journey, consider these final reflection questions to deepen your prayer practice and spiritual growth:

1. How has your understanding of prayer evolved throughout this journey?
2. What aspects of your prayer practice have brought you the most peace and fulfillment?
3. In what ways can you integrate gratitude, resilience, and forgiveness into your daily prayers?
4. How can you foster a sense of community and support through communal prayer?
5. What steps will you take to ensure that prayer remains a central part of your spiritual journey?

A Closing Prayer

Dear God,

Thank you for guiding us on this journey of prayer and spiritual discovery. As we conclude this exploration, we ask for your continued presence and guidance in our lives. Help us to embrace the power of prayer, to cultivate gratitude and resilience, and to practice forgiveness with a loving heart. May our prayers be a source of strength, healing, and inspiration, drawing us closer to you and to one another. Amen.

Moving Forward

As you move forward, may your journey of prayer be filled with moments of divine connection, profound insights, and spiritual growth. Remember that you are not alone; you are part of a greater community of faith that supports and uplifts you. Embrace the journey with an open heart and a spirit of love and compassion, knowing that each prayer brings you closer to the divine.

Thank you and may your path be blessed with peace, joy, and the unwavering presence of the divine.

Appendix A

Prayer Journal Template

Date: _____

Scripture Reading
Write down a Bible verse or passage you read today.

Reflection
Reflect on the scripture. What stood out to you? How does it apply to your life?

Prayer Requests
List your prayer requests for today.
1. _____
2. _____
3. _____

Prayers for Others
List the people you are praying for today.
1. _____
2. _____
3. _____

Personal Prayer
Write out your personal prayer to God, including praise, thanksgiving, confession, and requests.

Answered Prayers
Record any prayers that have been answered recently.

Reflection on the Day
How did God speak to you today? What insights did you gain?

Gratitude Journal Template

Date: _____

Three Things I Am Grateful For
  1. _____
  2. _____
  3. _____

Gratitude Reflection
Reflect on why you are grateful for these things. How do they impact your life positively?

Blessings of the Day
List any additional blessings you noticed today.

Gratitude Prayer
Write a prayer expressing your gratitude to God.

Positive Moments
Describe any positive moments or experiences you had today.

Personal Growth
Reflect on how practicing gratitude is affecting your attitude and outlook on life.

Forgiveness Log Template

Date: _____

Person to Forgive
Name or describe the person you are working to forgive.

Offense
Describe what happened that caused the hurt.

Feelings
Write down your feelings about the situation.

Steps to Forgiveness
1. Acknowledge the Hurt
   Describe how the offense impacted you emotionally and physically.
2. Empathize
   Try to understand the offender's perspective and reasons.
3. Decide to Forgive
   Make a conscious decision to forgive the person.
4. Release the Grudge
   Write down any steps you are taking to let go of the resentment.

Forgiveness Prayer
Write a prayer asking God for the strength to forgive and for healing from the hurt.

Positive Outcomes

Reflect on any positive changes you notice in your attitude or relationships as a result of forgiveness.

Follow-Up

Note any follow-up actions you need to take, such as communicating with the person or additional prayer.

Appendix B

Glossary

Adversity: Difficulties or misfortune. In the context of prayer and resilience, it refers to the challenges and hardships that one may face in life.

Amid: In the middle of or during. Example: "Praying for patience and understanding, while setting healthy boundaries, can help maintain a forgiving attitude even amid conflict."

Centering Prayer: A method of silent prayer that prepares you to experience God's presence. It involves sitting comfortably with eyes closed and silently introducing a sacred word or phrase to consent to God's presence.

Communal Prayer: The act of praying together with others, which strengthens bonds, fosters mutual support, and creates shared spiritual energy.

Compassion: Sympathetic pity and concern for the sufferings or misfortunes of others. In spiritual contexts, it often involves a deep feeling of sharing the suffering of another, coupled with a desire to relieve that suffering.

Contemplation: Deep reflective thought or the action of looking thoughtfully at something for a long time. In prayer, it refers to a profound level of meditation or reflection on the divine.

Divine: Of, from, or like God or a god. In the context of prayer, it refers to a higher power or the supreme being.

Emotional Flexibility: The ability to adapt to different emotional states and situations with ease, maintaining emotional balance.

Ephesians 4:32: A Bible verse that emphasizes kindness, compassion, and forgiveness, mirroring the forgiveness received from God.

Faith: Complete trust or confidence in someone or something. In spiritual terms, it refers to a strong belief in God or in the doctrines of a religion.

Forgiveness: The intentional and voluntary process of releasing feelings of resentment or vengeance toward someone who has wronged you.

Gratitude: The quality of being thankful; readiness to show appreciation for and to return kindness.

Guidance: Advice or information aimed at resolving a problem or difficulty, especially as given by someone in authority or someone knowledgeable.

Healing: The process of making or becoming sound or healthy again. In spiritual terms, it often refers to emotional or spiritual recovery.

Inner Peace: A state of mental and emotional calmness, with no anxiety, stress, or worry. In spiritual contexts, it is often associated with a deep sense of connection to the divine.

Lectio Divina: A traditional monastic practice of scriptural reading, meditation, and prayer intended to promote communion with God.

Mantra Meditation: A practice where a specific word or phrase (mantra) is repeated to focus the mind and enter a state of deep meditation.

Martin Luther King Jr.: A prominent leader in the American civil rights movement, known for his advocacy for nonviolent protest and his famous "I Have a Dream" speech.

Meditation: A practice where an individual uses a technique to focus their mind on a particular object, thought, or activity to achieve a mentally clear and emotionally calm state.

Nelson Mandela: A South African anti-apartheid revolutionary, political leader, and philanthropist who served as president of South Africa. Known for his resilience and commitment to justice and reconciliation.

Patience: The capacity to accept or tolerate delay, problems, or suffering without becoming annoyed or anxious.

Perseverance: Persistence in doing something despite difficulty or delay in achieving success.

Resilience: The capacity to recover quickly from difficulties; toughness. In the context of spiritual growth, it refers to the ability to withstand and grow from life's challenges.

Saint Teresa of Ávila: A Spanish noblewoman who became a Carmelite nun and author during the Counter-Reformation, known for her mystical writings and reforms of the Carmelite Order.

Spiritual Growth: The process of becoming more attuned to spiritual beliefs and practices, deepening one's connection with the divine.

Trust: Firm belief in the reliability, truth, ability, or strength of someone or something. In spiritual contexts, it often refers to faith in the divine.

Wisdom: The quality of having experience, knowledge, and good judgment. In spiritual terms, it often refers to insight gained through spiritual practice and connection with the divine.

Yoga: A group of physical, mental, and spiritual practices or disciplines which originated in ancient India. It is commonly practiced to promote physical and mental well-being.

Appendix C

Famous People Mentioned

1. **Helen Keller**: American author, political activist, and lecturer, known for being the first deaf-blind person to earn a bachelor of arts degree and her work advocating for people with disabilities.

Source: *The Story of My Life* by Helen Keller

2. **Jalal ad-Din Muhammad Rumi (Rumi)**: Persian poet, Islamic scholar, theologian, and Sufi mystic, known for his profound poetry and teachings on love and spirituality.

Famous Quote: "The wound is the place where the light enters you."

Source: *The Essential Rumi*, translated by Coleman Barks

3. **Martin Luther King Jr.**: American civil rights leader known for his nonviolent activism and leadership in the civil rights movement.

Famous Quotes
   o "Faith is taking the first step even when you don't see the whole staircase."
   o "Forgiveness is not an occasional act; it is a constant attitude."

Source: *Strength to Love* by Martin Luther King Jr.

4. **Mahatma Gandhi**: Leader of the Indian independence movement against British rule, known for his philosophy of nonviolent resistance.

Famous Quotes

o "Prayer is not asking. It is a longing of the soul. It is daily admission of one's weakness. It is better in prayer to have a heart without words than words without a heart."

o "The weak can never forgive. Forgiveness is the attribute of the strong."

Source: *The Essential Gandhi,* edited by Louis Fischer

5. **Nelson Mandela**: South African anti-apartheid revolutionary and political leader who served as president of South Africa from 1994 to 1999.

Source: *Long Walk to Freedom* by Nelson Mandela

6. **Saint Teresa of Ávila**: Spanish mystic, Roman Catholic saint, and author of spiritual classics such as "The Interior Castle" and "The Way of Perfection."

Source: *The Life of Saint Teresa of Ávila* by herself

7. **Jesus Christ**: Central figure of Christianity, whose teachings and life stories are recorded in the New Testament.

Source: The Holy Bible, New Testament

8. **Apostle Paul**: Early Christian missionary and writer of many of the New Testament epistles.

Source: The Holy Bible, New Testament

9. **Pope John Paul II**: Pope of the Catholic church from 1978 to 2005, known for his extensive travels and influence on the church's direction.

Source: *Witness to Hope: The Biography of Pope John Paul II* by George Weigel

10. **Lewis B. Smedes**: American Christian author, ethicist, and theologian known for his writings on forgiveness and moral issues.

Famous Quote: "To forgive is to set a prisoner free and discover that the prisoner was you."

Source: *Forgive and Forget: Healing the Hurts We Don't Deserve* by Lewis B. Smedes

Appendix D

Prayer of Forgiveness

Dear Heavenly Father,

I come before you today, seeking your grace and guidance. Your Word says, "Be kind and compassionate to one another, forgiving each other, just as in Christ God forgave you" (Ephesians 4:32). Lord, help me to embody this spirit of forgiveness in my own life.

I confess that I have held onto anger and resentment. I ask for your strength to forgive those who have wronged me. As your Word teaches, "If you forgive other people when they sin against you, your heavenly Father will also forgive you" (Matthew 6:14). Help me to release these burdens and embrace the freedom that comes from forgiving others.

Please cleanse my heart from bitterness and fill it with your love and peace. Teach me to see others through your eyes, with empathy and understanding. Heavenly Father, I also seek forgiveness for my own wrongdoings. I confess my sins before you and ask for Your mercy and cleansing.

In Jesus's name, I pray.

Amen.

Prayer of Gratitude

Dear Heavenly Father,

I come before you with a heart full of gratitude and praise. Your Word says, "Give thanks to the Lord for he is good; His love endures forever" (Psalm 107:1). I thank you for your endless love and grace in my life.

Lord, I am grateful for the many blessings you have bestowed upon me. "Every good and perfect gift is from above, coming down from the Father of the heavenly lights, who does not change like shifting shadows" (James 1:17). Thank you for the abundance of your gifts, both seen and unseen.

Help me to cultivate a grateful heart in all circumstances, knowing that your plans for me are good and perfect. Thank you for the gift of family and friends, for the love and support they provide. May I cherish these relationships and show appreciation for the people you have placed in my life.

Most of all, I thank you for the gift of salvation through your Son, Jesus Christ. May I live a life that reflects my gratitude for this incredible blessing.

In Jesus's name, I pray.

Amen.

Appendix E

Step-by-step Prayer Exercise

Prayer Exercise 1: Morning Gratitude and Intention Setting

Preparation
- Choose a quiet space where you can start your day with reflection.
- Have a journal or notepad and pen available.

Steps
1. Opening Prayer
- Begin with a simple prayer inviting God's presence.
- Example: "Dear God, thank you for the gift of this new day. Be with me as I begin my day, and guide my thoughts and actions. Amen."

2. Gratitude List
- Write down three things you are grateful for as you start your day.
- Reflect on why you are thankful for these blessings.

3. Scripture Reflection
- Read a Bible verse that inspires you for the day.
- Example: "This is the day the Lord has made; let us rejoice and be glad in it" (Psalm 118:24).
- Reflect on how this scripture can guide your day.

4. Setting Intentions
- Write down one or two intentions or goals for the day.
- Pray over these intentions, asking for guidance and strength.

-   Example: "Lord, help me to be patient and kind in my interactions today. Guide me to see and seize opportunities to serve others."

5. Silent Meditation
-   Spend a few moments in silent meditation, focusing on your breath and inviting peace into your heart.
-   Allow any worries or distractions to fade away.

6. Closing Prayer
-   End with a prayer of dedication for the day ahead.
-   Example: "Thank you, God, for this time of reflection. May my actions today reflect your love and grace. Amen."

Prayer Exercise 2: Evening Reflection and Forgiveness
Preparation
-   Find a quiet space where you can reflect on your day.
-   Have a journal or notepad and pen available.

Steps
1. Opening Prayer
-   Begin with a prayer inviting God's presence.
-   Example: "Heavenly Father, I come to you at the end of this day. Thank you for being with me through every moment. Amen."

2. Daily Reflection
-   Reflect on the events of your day.
-   Write down significant moments, both positive and challenging.

3. Scripture Reading
-   Read a Bible verse that speaks to reflection and forgiveness.
-   Example: "Be kind and compassionate to one another, forgiving each other, just as in Christ God forgave you" (Ephesians 4:32).
-   Reflect on how this scripture applies to your day.

4. Forgiveness Prayer

- Identify any moments where you felt hurt or where you hurt others.
- Pray for forgiveness and healing.
- Example: "Lord, I seek your forgiveness for any wrongs I have done today. Help me to forgive those who have hurt me and to seek reconciliation where needed. Heal my heart and grant me peace. Amen."

5. Gratitude and Blessings
- Write down three things you are thankful for from the day.
- Reflect on these blessings and offer a prayer of gratitude.
- Example: "Thank you, God, for the blessings of today. I am grateful for the kindness of friends, the beauty of nature, and the opportunities to learn and grow."

6. Silent Reflection
- Spend a few moments in silent reflection, inviting peace into your heart.
- Allow yourself to let go of any lingering stress or worries.

7. Closing Prayer
- End with a prayer of peace and rest.
- Example: "Thank you, God, for your presence and guidance today. Grant me a restful night and renew my spirit for the day ahead. Amen."

Prayer Exercise 3: Midday Pause and Renewal
Preparation
- Find a quiet space where you can take a short break.
- Have a small object of focus, like a cross or a piece of nature (e.g., a leaf, a stone).

Steps
1. Opening Prayer
- Begin with a prayer inviting God's presence into your break.

- Example: "Lord, I take this moment to pause and seek your presence. Renew my spirit and guide my thoughts. Amen."

2. Breathing Exercise
- Take a few deep breaths to center yourself.
- Focus on your breath, inhaling peace and exhaling stress.

3. Object Reflection
- Hold the object you chose and reflect on its significance.
- Use it as a focal point to connect with the divine.

4. Scripture Reading
- Read a short Bible verse that inspires peace and renewal.
- Example: "Come to me, all you who are weary and burdened, and I will give you rest" (Matthew 11:28).
- Reflect on how this scripture can bring renewal to your day.

5. Silent Meditation
- Spend a few moments in silent meditation, focusing on the scripture and your breath.
- Allow yourself to be present in the moment and feel God's peace.

6. Prayer for Strength
- Pray for strength and guidance for the rest of your day.
- Example: "Lord, thank you for this moment of peace. Grant me strength and clarity as I continue my day. Help me to carry your presence with me in all I do. Amen."

7. Closing Reflection
- Take a final deep breath and slowly return to your daily activities.
- Carry a sense of peace and renewal with you.

Appendix F

Interfaith Prayer Practices

Creating interfaith prayer practices involves recognizing and respecting the diverse spiritual traditions that people follow. These practices can foster understanding, unity, and mutual respect among individuals from different faith backgrounds. Here are some interfaith prayer practices that can be incorporated into communal gatherings or personal spiritual routines.

1. Shared Silence
    Purpose: To create a space for individuals of different faiths to come together in silent reflection or meditation.

    Practice
    -   Begin by inviting everyone to find a comfortable position.
    -   Introduce the shared silence by explaining that it is a time for personal reflection, meditation, or silent prayer according to each person's tradition.
    -   Set a timer for 5–10 minutes.
    -   End the silence with a gentle sound, such as a bell or chime.

Reflection: After the silence, invite participants to share their experiences or thoughts if they feel comfortable.

2. Reading Sacred Texts
    Purpose: To honor the wisdom found in various religious traditions by reading and reflecting on excerpts from sacred texts.

    Practice

- Choose short passages from different sacred texts, such as the Bible, Quran, Bhagavad Gita, Torah, and others.
- Read each passage aloud, pausing after each to allow for reflection.
- Invite participants to reflect on the common themes or values expressed in the readings.

Reflection: Encourage an open discussion where participants can share how the readings resonate with them personally.

3. Interfaith Blessings
   Purpose: To offer blessings from different faith traditions, fostering a sense of shared spirituality and goodwill.

   Practice
- Invite representatives from different faith communities to share a blessing or prayer from their tradition.
- Ensure that each blessing is inclusive and respectful of the diverse audience.
- Reflection: Allow time for participants to reflect on how they felt receiving blessings from various traditions.

4. Walking Meditation
   Purpose: To engage in a physical practice that promotes mindfulness and connection with the divine across different faiths.

   Practice
- Choose a serene outdoor location or a quiet indoor space where participants can walk slowly.
- Begin with a brief introduction to the concept of walking meditation, emphasizing mindfulness and presence.
- Walk in silence, paying attention to each step and the surrounding environment.

Reflection: After the walk, gather in a circle and invite participants to share their experiences.

5. Community Service as Prayer
   Purpose: To express shared values of compassion, service, and love through collective action.

   Practice
   - Organize a community service project, such as a food drive, environmental cleanup, or helping at a local shelter.
   - Begin the service activity with a moment of silence or a brief prayer from each represented faith.
   - Encourage participants to view their service as an act of prayer and devotion.

Reflection: After the service activity, gather to discuss the experience and the impact of working together.

6. Interfaith Chanting and Singing
   Purpose: To use music as a universal language that transcends religious differences and fosters unity.

   Practice
   - Choose simple, inclusive chants or songs from different traditions.
   - Teach the chants or songs to the group, encouraging participation.
   - Sing or chant together, focusing on the shared experience rather than the specific religious context.

Reflection: Invite participants to reflect on how the music affected their sense of connection and spirituality.

7. Joint Prayer for Peace
   Purpose: To unite in a common intention for peace and harmony in the world.

Practice
- Gather in a circle or a comfortable group setting.
- Begin with a moment of silence, inviting participants to hold peace in their hearts.
- Offer prayers for peace from various traditions, each followed by a moment of silent reflection.
- Conclude with a collective affirmation or intention for peace.

Reflection: Discuss how the act of praying for peace together can contribute to a sense of global unity and hope.

Example Interfaith Prayer

Opening

"We come together from diverse paths, united in our desire for peace, understanding, and love. In this shared space, may we honor each other's traditions and find common ground in our shared humanity."

Shared Silence
"Let us begin with a moment of silence, each of us connecting with our own faith and the divine presence."

Readings
- Bible: "Blessed are the peacemakers, for they shall be called children of God" (Matthew 5:9).
- Quran: "And make us a community of peace and submitters to you" (Quran 2:128).
- Bhagavad Gita: "He who has inner joy, who has inner peace, and in whom inner light shines—becomes the Spirit, and reaches the supreme aim of life in the Spirit" (Bhagavad Gita 5:24).

Interfaith Blessings
Representative from different faiths offer short prayers or blessings.

Joint Prayer for Peace

"May we all be blessed with peace, compassion, and understanding. May our hearts be open to love and our hands ready to serve. Together, we pray for a world where all can live in harmony."

Closing
"As we go forth from this gathering, may we carry the spirit of unity and peace with us, sharing it with all whom we meet."

Appendix G

Prayer Schedule

Morning Prayer Schedule
Goal: Start the day with gratitude, intention, and connection with God.

1. 6:00 AM—Wake Up and Stretch
    -   Begin with a gentle stretch and deep breathing to wake up your body.
    -   Thank God for the gift of a new day.
    -   Short prayer: "Lord, thank you for the gift of this new day. Fill me with your light and guide me throughout the day. Amen."

2. 6:10 AM—Morning Devotional
    -   Spend ten minutes reading a devotional or a passage from the Bible.
    -   Reflect on the reading and how it applies to your life.
    -   Example passage: "This is the day the Lord has made; let us rejoice and be glad in it" (Psalm 118:24).

3. 6:20 AM—Gratitude List
    -   Write down three things you are grateful for.
    -   Offer a prayer of thanks for each item on your list.
    -   Example: "Lord, I am grateful for my family, my health, and the opportunities you have provided. Thank you for your blessings. Amen."

4. 6:30 AM—Intention Setting
    -   Write down one or two intentions or goals for the day.
    -   Pray for guidance and strength to accomplish these goals.

- Example: "Lord, help me to be patient and kind today. Guide me to make wise decisions and to serve others with a loving heart. Amen."

5. 6:40 AM—Silent Meditation
- Spend 5–10 minutes in silent meditation, focusing on your breath and inviting God's presence into your day.
- Allow any worries or distractions to fade away.

6. 6:50 AM—Closing Prayer
- End with a prayer of dedication for the day ahead.
- Example: "Lord, thank you for this time of reflection and prayer. Be with me throughout the day and help me to live according to your will. Amen."

Afternoon Prayer Schedule
Goal: Pause and reconnect with God during the day for renewal and strength.

1. 12:00 PM—Midday Pause
- Find a quiet space to take a break from your activities.
- Take a few deep breaths to center yourself.

2. 12:05 PM—Scripture Reflection
- Read a short Bible verse that inspires peace and renewal.
- Example passage: "Come to me, all you who are weary and burdened, and I will give you rest" (Matthew 11:28).
- Reflect on how this scripture can bring renewal to your day.

3. 12:10 PM—Prayer for Strength
- Pray for strength and guidance for the rest of your day.
- Example: "Lord, thank you for this moment of peace. Grant me strength and clarity as I continue my day. Help me to carry your presence with me in all I do. Amen."

4. 12:15 PM—Silent Meditation

- Spend 5–10 minutes in silent meditation, focusing on your breath and the scripture you read.
- Allow yourself to be present in the moment and feel God's peace.

5. 12:25 PM—Gratitude Reflection
- Think of one thing that has gone well so far today.
- Offer a short prayer of thanks.
- Example: "Thank you, God, for the positive meeting this morning. I am grateful for your guidance and support. Amen."

6. 12:30 PM—Closing Reflection
- Take a final deep breath and slowly return to your daily activities.
- - Carry a sense of peace and renewal with you.

Evening Prayer Schedule
Goal: Reflect on the day, seek forgiveness, and find peace before bedtime.

1. 9:00 PM—Evening Reflection
- Find a quiet space to end your day in reflection.
- Light a candle or play soft instrumental music to create a peaceful atmosphere.

2. 9:05 PM—Daily Reflection
- Reflect on the events of your day.
- Write down significant moments, both positive and challenging.

3. 9:15 PM—Scripture Reading
- Read a Bible verse that speaks to reflection and forgiveness.
- Example passage: "Be kind and compassionate to one another, forgiving each other, just as in Christ God forgave you" (Ephesians 4:32).
- Reflect on how this scripture applies to your day.

4. 9:20 PM—Forgiveness Prayer

- Identify any moments where you felt hurt or where you hurt others.
- Pray for forgiveness and healing.
- Example: "Lord, I seek your forgiveness for any wrongs I have done today. Help me to forgive those who have hurt me and to seek reconciliation where needed. Heal my heart and grant me peace. Amen."

5. 9:30 PM—Gratitude and Blessings
- Write down three things you are thankful for from the day.
- Reflect on these blessings and offer a prayer of gratitude.
- Example: "Thank you, God, for the blessings of today. I am grateful for the kindness of friends, the beauty of nature, and the opportunities to learn and grow."

6. 9:40 PM—Silent Reflection
- Spend a few moments in silent reflection, inviting peace into your heart.
- Allow yourself to let go of any lingering stress or worries.

7. 9:50 PM—Closing Prayer
- End with a prayer of peace and rest.
- Example: "Thank you, God, for your presence and guidance today. Grant me a restful night and renew my spirit for the day ahead. Amen."

Appendix H

Biblical Verses and Inspirational Quotes

Additional Biblical Verses

1. Philippians 4:6–7 (NIV)

   Do not be anxious about anything, but in every situation, by prayer and petition, with thanksgiving, present your requests to God. And the peace of God, which transcends all understanding, will guard your hearts and your minds in Christ Jesus."

2. Jeremiah 29:11 (NIV)

   "For I know the plans I have for you, declares the Lord, plans to prosper you and not to harm you, plans to give you hope and a future."

3. Isaiah 40:31 (NIV)

   "But those who hope in the Lord will renew their strength. They will soar on wings like eagles; they will run and not grow weary, they will walk and not be faint."

Additional Inspirational Quotes

1. Mahatma Gandhi

   "The best way to find yourself is to lose yourself in the service of others."

2. Helen Keller

   "Alone we can do so little; together we can do so much."

3. Rumi

   "The wound is the place where the light enters you."

Appendix I

Frequently Asked Questions (FAQ)

1. What is the purpose of this book?

    Answer: The purpose of this book is to guide readers on a journey of prayer and spiritual growth. It aims to provide practical insights, techniques, and reflections to deepen their prayer practice, enhance their connection with the divine, and explore themes such as gratitude, resilience, forgiveness, and community in prayer.

2. Who is this book intended for?

    Answer: This book is intended for anyone seeking to deepen their prayer practice and spiritual life. It is suitable for individuals from various faith traditions, as well as those who are new to prayer or looking to explore different aspects of spirituality.

3. How can I incorporate the prayer techniques mentioned in the book into my daily routine?

    Answer: To incorporate the prayer techniques into your daily routine, start by setting aside a specific time each day for prayer. Experiment with different techniques, such as silent meditation or gratitude prayers, to see which resonate most with you. Consistency is key, so aim to make prayer a regular part of your day, whether in the morning, evening, or during breaks.

4. What if I am new to prayer and don't know where to start?

    Answer: If you are new to prayer, begin by setting aside a few minutes each day for quiet reflection or meditation. Start with simple prayers of gratitude or asking for guidance. As you become more comfortable, explore different prayer techniques mentioned in the book, such as centering prayer or mantra meditation. Remember, there is no right or wrong way to pray—it's about finding what feels meaningful and authentic to you.

5. How can I create a personalized prayer schedule?

Answer: To create a personalized prayer schedule, consider your daily routine and identify times when you can dedicate a few moments to prayer. It could be in the morning, during lunch breaks, or before bedtime. Choose prayer techniques that resonate with you and align with your spiritual goals. Write down your schedule and try to stick to it, adjusting as needed to fit your lifestyle.

6. What are some interfaith prayer practices that I can incorporate into my spiritual routine?

Answer: Interfaith prayer practices include shared silence, reading sacred texts from various traditions, offering interfaith blessings, engaging in walking meditation, participating in community service, chanting or singing interfaith songs, and holding joint prayers for peace. These practices can help you connect with others from different faith backgrounds and foster a sense of unity and mutual respect.

7. How can I practice forgiveness in prayer?

Answer: Practicing forgiveness in prayer involves seeking divine assistance to let go of resentment and anger. Start by praying for strength and guidance to forgive those who have wronged you. Reflect on your feelings and ask for healing. Consider including prayers of gratitude to shift your focus from hurt to healing. Remember that forgiveness is a process that takes time and patience.

8. How do I deepen my prayer practice through gratitude?

    Answer: To deepen your prayer practice through gratitude, start by incorporating gratitude prayers into your daily routine. Begin or end your prayer sessions by thanking the divine for specific blessings in your life. Keep a gratitude journal where you write down things you are thankful for each day. This practice helps shift your focus from what you lack to the abundance in your life, enhancing your spiritual connection.

9. How can I join or start a communal prayer group?

    Answer: To join a communal prayer group, check with local places of worship, community centers, or online platforms for existing groups. If you want to start a group, invite friends, family, or community members to join you. Set a regular meeting time and place, and decide on a structure for your prayer sessions. Ensure that the group is inclusive and respectful of different faith traditions.

10. What should I do if I struggle with maintaining a consistent prayer practice?

    Answer: If you struggle with maintaining a consistent prayer practice, start small and be patient with yourself. Set realistic goals, such as dedicating just a few minutes each day to prayer. Use reminders or set a specific time for prayer to create a routine. Explore different prayer techniques to keep your practice engaging and meaningful. Seek support from a prayer group or spiritual mentor to stay motivated and accountable.

11. How can I use this book to enhance my spiritual journey?

Answer: Use this book as a guide and resource for your spiritual journey. Follow the chapters to explore different aspects of prayer, and try the suggested techniques and practices. Reflect on the questions and exercises provided to deepen your understanding and connection with the divine. Personalize your prayer practice by integrating the insights and methods that resonate with you, and revisit the book as needed for inspiration and guidance.

Appendix J

Reflection Questions

Chapter 1: Understanding Prayer

1. How has your understanding of prayer evolved over time?
    Answer: My understanding of prayer has evolved from seeing it as a formal ritual to recognizing it as a dynamic conversation with the divine. I now see prayer as a way to connect deeply with my spiritual beliefs and to find guidance and solace in my daily life.

2. What role does prayer play in your daily life?
    Answer: Prayer plays a central role in my daily life by providing a sense of peace and direction. It helps me start and end my day with gratitude and reflection, keeping me grounded and mindful throughout my activities.

3. How do you experience the creator's presence during prayer?
    Answer: I experience the creator's presence during prayer through a profound sense of peace and clarity. Sometimes it feels like a quiet assurance or a comforting presence that reassures me I am not alone.

4. In what ways has prayer influenced your spiritual journey?
    Answer: Prayer has been a guiding force in my spiritual journey, helping me navigate challenges, find purpose, and deepen my faith. It has strengthened my connection with the divine and provided insights into my life's path.

Chapter 2: The Importance of Prayer

1. Why is prayer important in our spiritual lives?
   Answer: Prayer is important because it fosters a direct connection with the divine, allowing us to express our hopes, fears, gratitude, and needs. It nurtures our spiritual growth and helps us align our lives with our values and beliefs.

2. How can prayer influence our daily actions and decisions?
   Answer: Prayer can provide clarity and discernment, helping us make decisions that are aligned with our spiritual values. It also cultivates a sense of inner peace that influences how we interact with others and handle daily challenges.

3. What benefits have you experienced from maintaining a regular prayer practice?
   Answer: Maintaining a regular prayer practice has brought me a sense of stability, peace, and purpose. It has helped me manage stress, find comfort in difficult times, and cultivate a more grateful and positive outlook on life.

4. How does prayer help you navigate life's challenges?
   Answer: Prayer helps me navigate life's challenges by offering a space to seek guidance, find strength, and maintain hope. It reminds me that I am supported by a higher power and helps me stay resilient in the face of adversity.

Chapter 3: Developing a Prayer Practice

1. What steps have you taken to establish a regular prayer practice?
   Answer: I have set aside specific times each day for prayer, created a dedicated space for reflection, and incorporated various prayer techniques to keep my practice engaging. Consistency and commitment have been key to establishing this routine.

2. How do you stay motivated to maintain your prayer practice?

Answer: I stay motivated by reflecting on the positive impact prayer has on my life and by setting realistic goals. Integrating prayer into my daily routine also helps maintain my motivation.

3. What challenges have you faced in developing a consistent prayer routine, and how have you overcome them?
    Answer: One challenge has been finding the time in the middle of a busy schedule. I have overcome this by prioritizing prayer and incorporating it into my daily activities, such as through short moments of mindfulness or gratitude prayers throughout the day.

4. How has your prayer practice evolved over time?
    Answer: My prayer practice has evolved from sporadic and formal prayers to a more integrated and dynamic routine. I now use a variety of techniques, including meditation and journaling to deepen my spiritual connection.

Chapter 4: Deepening Your Prayer Practice

1. Which new prayer technique have you found most enriching, and why?
    Answer: I have found Lectio Divina most enriching because it combines scripture reading with meditation and contemplation, allowing me to deeply engage with sacred texts and find personal meaning in them.

2. How has incorporating movement into your prayer practice affected your spiritual experience?
    Answer: Incorporating movement, such as yoga or walking meditation, has made my prayer practice more holistic and embodied. It helps me connect my physical, mental, and spiritual selves, creating a more profound and integrated experience.

3. What role does creativity play in deepening your prayer practice?

Answer: Creativity, through activities like drawing, or writing, has allowed me to express my spirituality in new and meaningful ways. It has opened up different avenues for reflection and connection with the divine.

4. How do you balance different prayer techniques to maintain a dynamic prayer life?
Answer: I balance different prayer techniques by being flexible and responsive to my spiritual needs. I rotate techniques based on what feels most nourishing at the time, ensuring that my practice remains dynamic and fulfilling.

Chapter 5: Cultivating Inner Stillness

1. What benefits have you experienced from incorporating periods of silence into your prayer practice?
Answer: Periods of silence have brought a deep sense of peace and clarity. They help me quiet my mind, listen more intently to divine guidance, and connect with my inner self on a profound level.

2. How do you create intentional spaces for solitude in your daily life?
Answer: I create spaces for solitude by setting aside specific times for reflection, choosing quiet environments, and minimizing distractions. This intentional practice helps me find moments of peace amid the busyness of life.

3. How does practicing mindfulness enhance your prayer experience?
Answer: Mindfulness enhances my prayer experience by keeping me present and fully engaged. It helps me savor each moment, deepen my awareness of God's presence, and cultivate a more grateful and attentive heart.

4. In what ways has inner stillness influenced your spiritual growth?
Answer: Inner stillness has allowed me to hear the subtle whispers of divine guidance, fostering a deeper sense of trust and faith. It has also helped me develop greater patience, resilience, and a more contemplative approach to life.

Chapter 6: Embracing Gratitude in Prayer

1. How does practicing gratitude in prayer impact your overall well-being?
Answer: Practicing gratitude in prayer enhances my overall well-being by shifting my focus to the positive aspects of my life. It helps me cultivate a joyful and contented spirit, reducing stress and fostering a sense of abundance.

2. Can you recall a specific instance where expressing gratitude in prayer changed your perspective?
Answer: During a challenging period at work, expressing gratitude in prayer helped me focus on the support and opportunities I had rather than the difficulties. This shift in perspective brought a sense of peace and optimism.

3. How can you incorporate mindful gratitude practices into your daily life?
Answer: I incorporate mindful gratitude practices by keeping a gratitude journal, expressing thanks during meals, and taking moments throughout the day to silently acknowledge the blessings around me.

4. How does gratitude deepen your connection with the divine?
Answer: Gratitude deepens my connection with the divine by fostering a sense of reverence and appreciation for God's presence in my life. It opens my heart to receive and recognize the many ways I am blessed.

Chapter 7: Nurturing Resilience Through Prayer

1. What specific experiences have tested your resilience, and how did prayer help you navigate those challenges?
   Answer: A major health crisis tested my resilience, and prayer provided the strength and hope I needed to persevere. It helped me find peace in the midst of uncertainty and trust in a higher plan.

2. How can you develop a more consistent prayer practice to strengthen your resilience?
   Answer: I can develop a more consistent prayer practice by setting regular times for prayer, seeking accountability through a prayer partner or group, and integrating prayer into daily routines to build resilience.

3. In what ways has prayer helped you find meaning in suffering?
   Answer: Prayer has helped me find meaning in suffering by offering a space to reflect on my experiences and seek understanding. It has taught me valuable lessons about compassion, strength, and the transformative power of faith.

4. How does embracing resilience through prayer impact your spiritual journey?
   Answer: Embracing resilience through prayer has strengthened my faith and trust in God's guidance. It has empowered me to face challenges with courage and grace, knowing that I am supported by a divine presence.

Chapter 8: The Role of Community in Prayer

1. How has participating in communal prayer strengthened your sense of connection to your faith community?
   Answer: Participating in communal prayer has strengthened my sense of connection by fostering a sense of belonging and

mutual support. It has provided opportunities to share and grow together in faith.

2. What benefits have you experienced from praying with others?
Answer: Praying with others has brought a sense of shared purpose, encouragement, and spiritual energy. It has deepened my understanding of community and enhanced my personal prayer practice.

3. How can you offer support and encouragement to others through communal prayer?
Answer: I can offer support and encouragement by listening to others' needs and praying for their intentions. Being present and compassionate fosters a supportive prayer community.

4. In what ways can communal prayer provide comfort and strength during times of difficulty?
Answer: Communal prayer provides comfort and strength by creating a collective space of hope and solidarity. Knowing that others are praying for you and with you can be profoundly reassuring and empowering.

Chapter 9: The Power of Forgiveness in Prayer

1. What past hurts or grievances are you holding onto, and how can prayer help you release them?
Answer: I have held onto past grievances with a former superiors and former friend. Prayer has help me release these hurts and continues to help me by offering a space to seek divine strength and guidance for forgiveness, fostering a sense of peace and letting go.

2. How has the act of forgiving someone positively impacted your life and spiritual growth?

Answer: Forgiving loved ones for past wrongs has brought immense relief and healing. It has deepened my spiritual growth by teaching me compassion, empathy, and the liberating power of forgiveness.

3. In what ways can you seek forgiveness from those you may have wronged?
   Answer: I can seek forgiveness by acknowledging my mistakes, offering sincere apologies, and making amends where possible. Praying for courage and humility can support this process of reconciliation.

4. How does self-compassion play a role in your journey of self-forgiveness?
   Answer: Self-compassion allows me to acknowledge my imperfections and mistakes without harsh self-judgment. It plays a crucial role in self-forgiveness by fostering kindness and understanding toward myself, enabling healing and growth.

Appendix K

References for Prayer Techniques

Religious Texts

1. The Bible: For Christian prayer techniques.
2. The Quran: For Islamic prayer practices.
3. The Bhagavad Gita: For Hindu prayer techniques.
4. The Dhammapada: For Buddhist prayer practices.
5. The Torah: For Jewish prayer techniques.

Writings by Spiritual Leaders

1. St. Teresa of Ávila: For Christian contemplative prayer.
   - *The Interior Castle* by St. Teresa of Ávila
2. Rumi: For Sufi prayer and meditation.
   - *The Essential Rumi*, translated by Coleman Barks
3. Thomas Merton: For Christian monastic prayer.
   - *New Seeds of Contemplation* by Thomas Merton

Scholarly Articles and Books

1. Richard J. Foster: For a broad overview of Christian prayer practices.
   - *Prayer: Finding the Heart's True Home* by Richard J. Foster
2. Eknath Easwaran: For meditation and prayer techniques from various traditions.
   - *Passage Meditation* by Eknath Easwaran
3. Thich Nhat Hanh: For Buddhist mindfulness and prayer.
   - *The Miracle of Mindfulness* by Thich Nhat Hanh

Historical and Cultural Studies

1. Mircea Eliade: For the history of religious practices.
   - *The Sacred and the Profane: The Nature of Religion* by Mircea Eliade
2. Huston Smith: For comparative religion.
   - *The World's Religions* by Huston Smith

Modern Spiritual Guides

1. Henri Nouwen: For insights into Christian prayer and spirituality.
   - *The Way of the Heart* by Henri Nouwen
2. Wayne Teasdale: For interfaith prayer practices.
   - *The Mystic Heart: Discovering a Universal Spirituality in the World's Religions* by Wayne Teasdale

Additional Specific Techniques

1. Yoga and Mantra Meditation
   - Easwaran, Eknath. *Passage Meditation*. Nilgiri Press, 1978.
   - Vivekananda, Swami. *Raja Yoga*. Advaita Ashrama, 1896.

2. Centering Prayer
   - Keating, Thomas. *Open Mind, Open Heart: The Contemplative Dimension of the Gospel*. Continuum, 1986.
   - Pennington, Basil. *Centering Prayer: Renewing an Ancient Christian Prayer Form*. Image, 1980.

3. Lectio Divina
   - Benedict, St. *The Rule of St. Benedict*. Multiple editions.
   - Nouwen, Henri. *Spiritual Formation: Following the Movements of the Spirit*. HarperOne, 2010.

4. The Examen:
   - Ignatius of Loyola, St. *The Spiritual Exercises of St. Ignatius*. Multiple editions.

- Martin, James. *The Jesuit Guide to (Almost) Everything: A Spirituality for Real Life*. HarperOne, 2010.

5. Prayer with Icons:
   - Nouwen, Henri. *Behold the Beauty of the Lord: Praying with Icons*. Ave Maria Press, 1987.
   - Baggley, John. *Prayer and Icon*. St. Vladimir's Seminary Press, 1987.

References

- St. Padre Pio
    - o Pio, St. Padre. *Words of Light: Inspiration from the Letters of Padre Pio.* Paraclete Press, 2009.

- John Wesley
    - o Wesley, John. *The Works of John Wesley.* Baker Books, 2007.

- Martin Luther King Jr.
    - o King Jr., Martin Luther. *Strength to Love.* Harper & Row, 1963.
    - o King Jr., Martin Luther. *A Testament of Hope: The Essential Writings and Speeches.* Edited by James M. Washington, HarperOne, 1986.

- Buddha
    - o Buddha. *The Dhammapada.* Translated by Eknath Easwaran, Nilgiri Press, 1985.

- Mahatma Gandhi
    - o Gandhi, Mahatma. *A Simple Path.* Ballantine Books, 1995.

- Søren Kierkegaard
  - o Kierkegaard, Søren. *Provocations: Spiritual Writings of Kierkegaard*. Edited by Charles E. Moore, Plough Publishing House, 2002.

- Mother Teresa
  - o Teresa, Mother. *A Simple Path*. Ballantine Books, 1995.

- Philippians 4:6
  - o The Holy Bible, New International Version. *Philippians 4:6*. Zondervan, 2011.

- Oswald Chambers
  - o Chambers, Oswald. *My Utmost for His Highest*. Barbour Publishing, 1935.

- Matthew 18:20
  - o The Holy Bible, New International Version. *Matthew 18:20*. Zondervan, 2011.

- Lewis B. Smedes
  - o Smedes, Lewis B. *Forgive and Forget: Healing the Hurts We Don't Deserve*. HarperOne, 1984.

- Jalal ad-Din Muhammad Rumi
  - o Quote: "The wound is the place where the light enters you."
  - o Reference: Rumi, Jalaluddin. *The Essential Rumi*. Translated by Coleman Barks, HarperOne, 1995.

About the Author

Roxie Dantzler, began a profound healing journey that served as the inspiration for this book. Through the process of healing and self-discovery, Ms. Dantzler gained invaluable insights and wisdom that she believes are meant to be shared with others. Her dedication to personal growth and spiritual exploration is at the heart of this work.

With a professional background that includes serving as a dental assistant in the US Army as well as roles in program analysis and human resources management, Ms. Dantzler brings a unique perspective to the themes of journeying to the heart with prayer, resilience, and spiritual practice. These diverse experiences have enriched her understanding of the human experience and the ways in which we can connect with the divine.

Outside of writing, Ms. Dantzler finds peace and inspiration by listening to the ocean while relaxing on the beach. This hobby provides a serene backdrop for reflection and spiritual contemplation, further influencing her writing and approach to life.

Throughout her professional and personal life, Ms. Dantzler's journey has been marked by a commitment to exploring the depths of spirituality and fostering a connection with the divine. Her personal experiences have profoundly influenced the themes in this book, making it a heartfelt guide for those seeking deeper spiritual connection and personal growth.

Through this book, Ms. Dantzler aims to convey a message of hope, resilience, and the transformative power of prayer. She believes that sharing knowledge and wisdom can illuminate the path for others, helping them navigate their own journeys with grace and understanding.

Roxie Dantzler

Printed in the USA
CPSIA information can be obtained
at www.ICGtesting.com
LVHW011307290824
789617LV00005BA/152/J

9 798369 427552